Out of Business

Force a company, business, or store,
to close its doors... for good!

Out of Business

Force a company, business, or store to close its doors... for good!

by Dennis Fiery

Loompanics Unlimited
Port Townsend, Washington

Out of Business

Force a company, business, or store to close its doors... for good!

© 1999 by Dennis Fiery

Published by:
Loompanics Unlimited
PO Box 1197
Port Townsend, WA 98368
Loompanics Unlimited is a division of Loompanics Enterprises, Inc.
1-360-385-2230
E-mail: loompanx@olympus.net
Web site: www.loompanics.com

Art by Jim Blanchard

ISBN 1-55950-190-1
Library of Congress Card Catalog 98-89028

Table of Contents

About the Author

Dennis Fiery was born in 1972 to semi-hippie parents. After crisscrossing the country he settled down on the East Coast where he enjoys the close proximity of many bustling cities. He has worked for several crummy corporations that plummeted down the toilet and out of business, leaving him jobless. From those experiences he learned what makes companies fail. He is currently at peace with the world, except for the IRS and insurance companies, and enjoys inline skating, museums, bicycling, jet skiing, and drunken revelry.

"*For over 20 years I have peed on nasty corporations, companies and businesses. Now here comes Dennis Fiery to drown them with this 10,000-gallon Superpissoaker of a book.*

"*Great how-to in a hilarious step-by-step fashion. Fiery's book will truly piss off the censorious pissants of government and big business. And that's the good news. There's no bad news.*

"*If I weren't me, I'd swear that Dennis Fiery could out-hayduke Hayduke. He misses no deserved targets.*"

— George Hayduke, author of *Get Even* and other revenge books, and Dean of the College of Creative Revenge

By the Way...

1. The memos, e-mails, computer files, and letters reproduced throughout this book are real. They have been culled from actual offices and businesses of all types. However, all names have been changed to protect the innocent.

2. Web pages go up and down faster than a Times Square hooker. All web sites, phone numbers, e-mail addresses, and all the rest of it was accurate at time of publication. If it ain't there when you look, look a little harder. You're sure to find another new page that does the same thing as the one that went down.

3. The information in this book is presented for informational purposes only, and is intended to aid business owners who wish to keep their businesses safe and secure and raking in dough. The author and publisher assume no responsibility for use or misuse of this information. You have your own brain — use it!

Icon Key:

📖	Books
🛍	Shoppers
🖥	Computer web pages
☎	Telephone numbers

Introduction

by Victor Santoro
Author of *Gaslighting, Techniques of Revenge,*
Economic Sodomy, and *The Rip-Off Book*

This book is for people who hate businesses and business people, written by someone who hates them. Maybe you know the author. He could be your neighbor, or the guy down the block or in the next office. He might even be you!

Why do so many people hate businesses? That's a no-brainer. We see businesses as the economic giants who trample little people in the pursuit of profits. Big businesses set high prices, high rates, and dictate the terms of purchases. We're forced to buy electricity from one company, "regulated" by public officials who are bought and paid for by the business they "regulate." We have a choice of long distance telephone carriers, but in any area there is only one local telephone company, take it or leave it.

Businesses also force upon us their programs of aggressive commercialism. They flood our mailboxes with advertisements, so-called "junk mail." Not content merely to dump their ads into our mailboxes, they cunningly disguise their envelopes to make us open them. Some look like government window envelopes, and the literature inside looks like a check.

Other junk mail ads promise us on the outside envelope that we "HAVE ALREADY WON" a contest, but when we open it and begin reading the fine print we see that we've "won" up to the "finalist" stage, along with 100,000 other people.

Are you on the Internet? That's where you see aggressive commercialism at its worst. Try to gain access to almost any web site, say one that provides stock market quotes, and notice how the advertising banners always download before the data you're seeking. You sometimes have to scroll through several screens of ads that clog up bandwidth and slow downloads to a crawl before you get to the information you're seeking. Also, notice how in many cases the top and bottom of your screen are permanently filled with four-color ads, even animated ads, leaving you with a stingy little two-inch box for your data.

Of course, radio and TV have long been polluted by ads. Watch a movie on a commercial station and you'll see how they've cut the movie to fit in ads. Also, they'll let the movie play uninterrupted for a half hour or so at the start, to get you hooked. However, during the last half hour, you'll find four minutes of movie alternating with five minutes of ads.

Every day, we see billboards, benches, walls, buses, trains, windows, etc. polluted by these commercial graffiti, all of them clamoring for your attention. Pick up a magazine, and you'll find some ads printed on stiff paper, to make the magazine fall open at that page. Articles begin in the front, then are carefully threaded through the back pages, to expose you to as many ads as possible as you follow the story.

Now these are only the aspects you can ignore. If you're like most of us, and work for a business, you'll find out very quickly that you're very expendable, and that loyalty is strictly a one-way street. Your boss expects you to give him two weeks' notice when you plan to change jobs. However, when it's time for "downsizing," you're lucky to get an hour's notice. Adding insult to injury is the increasingly common practice of having a security guard escort you to your desk, to make sure you're packing only personal belongings, then out to the gate.

When a top executive decides that your salary is standing in the way of a more profitable bottom line, your twenty years of faithful service go right down the toilet. The many times you came in sick because you knew your boss needed you no longer count when it comes time to can you.

That's where this book comes in handy. If you work for one of these bosses from hell, and you see the handwriting on the wall, you don't have to walk to the garbage can passively. As an insider, and by following the tactics outlined in this book, you can create so much havoc that your boss will lose a lot of money, and may even have to close his doors.

This book should really have been titled "The Encyclopedia of Anti-Business Tactics," because it's so comprehensive. The author knows that not all tactics can work against all businesses, so he systematizes vulnerabilities and lists the tactics that work against them. You could force a product recall in a company that makes toasters or bicycles, but you couldn't do that against a lawyer or an insurance company. However, you can squirt super glue into their locks, place fake ads, interfere with their telephone system, divert their mail, place phony telephone calls, and use many other dirty tricks against them.

As the author points out, you don't even have to be an employee to make these tactics work, although the advantage of being an "insider" is indisputable. You can subscribe the company's e-mail address to a lot of mailing lists that will clog up its e-mail just as junk mail clogs your mailbox. The author shows how networking can supply you with lots of inside information, which you can use to plan your destructive campaign. Just the name of a vice-president and that of her school-age son are enough. You telephone her office and say:

"This is Officer Calhoun. Please tell Mrs. Smith that her son John's been injured in an accident and that we're taking him to Mercy Hospital right now. Tell her to ask for me at the hospital."

That's all. Even if Vice President Smith checks with the school before going to the hospital, the knowledge that someone would play such a cruel trick will take the starch out of her that day. Worse, she'll be wondering what might happen next, and if she's got a lively imagination, she'll lie awake at night thinking of all the ways her vulnerabilities might be attacked.

So it goes. Today's businesses are so complex and dependent on so many complex services that they have many vulnerabilities. Diverting the mail can put a serious crimp in the cash flow as checks take the slow route to Bangor, Maine or Fairbanks, Alaska. Placing phony ads that result in many telephone calls in response can tie up a company's telephone lines or e-mail for hours or days.

So pore through the pages of this book with a serious purpose, but be ready for laughs. Like the books on harassment, this one is funny. Learn how you can mess up an employer by attacking his advertising, his fax machine, e-mail system, travel plans, etc. Read how the boss's customer relations are vulnerable to disruption, if you plan your attack correctly. Find out how to bypass the employer's security, and bore to the core of the business to plant your monkey-wrench. Best of all, learn how to have fun while doing it.

Fragile Businesses

Businesses are fragile things. Look at those harried, frenzied executives in their dark suits and worried expressions. They know in their hearts that even the largest companies are destined to fall at any moment. Small businesses can fail because they don't have enough capital to keep going, they don't have enough customers, or they don't have enough workers to carry the workload. Big businesses have the opposite problem: too much money wasted on stupid employees who make mistakes and don't get the job done, they throw money around without rhyme or reason, and the company stays on its course because if anything *really* goes wrong they can always lay off a thousand workers to raise some fast cash. But in all kinds of businesses, large and small, we find the same problems and foibles, and a number of soft spots where we can attack. And attack we shall, with relish! That's what this book is about — 101 methods to attack a business, to make it go out of business.

There are three kinds of attacks: Money, Mental, and Reputation:

- **Money attacks** are those which cause the business to lose money. If you continuously cause the business to waste money, it must eventually run dry.

- **Mental attacks** go at the employees of the firm. You'll need employees who are dejected, stressed out, and overworked. Demoralized employees create costly mistakes. They tend to leave in a huff, which costs the company money to replace them. And if they really hate the company they might join forces with you to attack it to the ground.

- **Reputation attacks** go for the customer angle. When you attack the company's reputation, the customers run away in droves. If your target is a consulting group, you'd especially want to spring lots of reputation attacks against them, for their reputation is what draws clients. Might even be worthwhile to hire a detective (or become your own detective) to dig up dirt on them.

Sometimes these attacks overlap. If you attack the company's reputation, it will lose customers, and therefore lose money as well. The employees might therefore lose their motivation to work, and the company starts a downward spiral out of control. If you keep attacking the company using a combination of tactics, you will be helping the company closer to its grave with every action you take.

"Why would I want to force a company out of business?"

There are too many businesses in the world, they're getting too cocky, and the less we have the better. You might have your own personal reasons for wanting a particular company to close its doors.

- **They're morally reprehensible.** Maybe the company is morally offensive to you, because it espouses meat-eating, abortion, anti-religious views, pro-religious views, animal testing, racism, or whatever cause makes your blood boil.

- **They've done you wrong.** Perhaps the company has screwed you in some way and you want to return the favor. Insurance companies would get my vote in this category.

- **They're competing with you.** Or maybe you want that business to fail because they are your direct competitors, and with them out of the picture your own company would flourish.

So, do you have a grudge? Have a gripe? Whatever the reason, I wish you well in your campaign to close those corporate doors — for good!

"What kinds of businesses are we talking about here?"

In general we're talking about *any* company or business. It can be an office building, a retail store, a lemonade stand, a consulting firm, a giant known round the world, or a fledgling business just starting out. The techniques can also be used against other organizations, like clubs, non-profit groups, and schools. Some of the techniques target specific things like advertising or the company's booth at a trade show. Obviously if the company does not advertise or attend trade shows, those techniques can't be used against them. But taken as a whole, there are a lot of ideas here, so you should be able to find quite a few that can be used against your target company.

"Can I really do this?"

If you're dedicated, I'm sure you can. But keep in mind, it will take a lot of work on your part to really force a business to close its doors. It might even be a full time job for you! After all, you will be struggling against a whole company full of people whose sole purpose is to oppose your efforts. *Each person who works for the company is working against your efforts to force it out of business.* That's why it's crucial, if you're serious about this, to gather together a team of warriors who will fight on your side. But even if you don't force the company out of business, you will find it worthwhile to use some of the techniques every once in a while just to get your point across.

For instance, if you run a competing business, you might want to choose some tactics to kill their Christmas sales (and increase your own). Or if you're out for revenge, it may be enough to screw them out of the same amount of money that they screwed out of you. So even if you're not out for the kill, it can be fruitful to plan mini-attacks and win the battles that present themselves from time to time.

Let's Begin!

This book could be called *101 Things You Can Do To Destroy a Company.* Following are 101 techniques to wreak havoc against your least favorite company. The techniques are grouped thematically (a section on travel, a section on trade shows, a section on meetings, etc). Within each grouping there is a combination of the three forms of attack: money, mental, and reputation. You will find out about real-life instances of people who used these techniques, and we will investigate how you can learn from their mistakes so your own attacks go off without a hitch. Throughout the book there will also be a series of Special Tactic Reports where we will discuss other pertinent topics such as how to gather a team of people to fight the company, how to gain access to the premises, and sneaky methods of industrial espionage. By the end of this book you will have been exposed to a diabolical smorgasbord of all sorts. Many of these ideas are illegal, dangerous, amoral, and not conducive to landing you in heaven.

That's why they're so much fun.

Anyone, Anyplace, Anywhere

Let's start with some general attacks that can be used against any company.

Attack #1. Rampant Rumors

Rumors can be used to send consumers running away to the competition. The fact is, many consumers are extremely stupid. They believe idiotic rumors like Proctor & Gamble is in league with the devil, and not only do they believe it — they boycott it! What's that all about, you wonder? In 1980 a rumor started circulating that corporate giant Proctor & Gamble was somehow linked to Satanism; the company was run by devil worshippers, and it donated 10 percent of its income to Satanic groups.[1] At the time P & G's logo was a crescent moon and thirteen stars. This angered folks in the Bible Belt to no end. (Some of those folks should loosen the belt because it's cutting off circulation to the brain.) But they believed it through-and-throughout. By the spring of 1982, the Proctor & Gamble toll-free lines were fielding twelve thousand calls a month on the silly topic. Consumers threatened boycotts against the products and the stores who carried the products, and there were even reports of attacks against P & G employees and their automobiles. The company eventually enacted lawsuits against some people identified as spreading the rumor.[2]

Imagine you're an executive at Proctor & Gamble. You're trying to dream up newfangled ways to sell toothpaste to the public, and for no particular reason you've suddenly got *all that* to deal with. Statements have to be made, damage control has to be done, ads must be written up, placed, and paid for, attorneys contacted and exorbitant attorney fees paid. Even though you're completely innocent, you have to run around as if you're guilty of something!

The number of corporate rumors that have appeared in recent years is staggering. Did you hear the one about Bubble Yum bubble gum containing spider eggs? The Life Savers company had to take out full-page newspaper ads in 1977 to suppress this rumor. (And even that didn't completely work. I remember being in summer camp years later when another camper informed me that the gum contains beetle doody.)

General Foods also took out full-page ads when gossip circulated that Pop Rocks candy explodes in the stomach and causes cancer. There have been rumors that McDonald's adds red worms to its hamburgers,[3] and the list doesn't end there. (Let's go on with this because it's a good way to generate ideas you can use against your own target company.) Back in the '40s, the breakfast cereal Force was rumored to contain morphine, which agitated the company no end.[4] Various food companies (usually beer, liquor, tomato products, and sauces) have been the targets of rumors that a worker fell into a vat of the stuff and drowned there. Coca-Cola, of all companies, was hit by this rumor in 1981 in the Far East to such an extent that sales of Coke began to drop. So concerned were they, that an industry association issued a press release and placed ads in local newspapers to explain the truth.[5]

Rumors with political or social themes can cause even more economic hardships to the firm, because there are political and religious groups with money who will spend it against the corporation. And if not that, these themes are broad enough to outrage many consumers. In the mid-to-late 1970s, Anheuser-Busch brewery and later, the Coors company, suffered misery when rumors circulated that those companies donated money to support gun control legislation. In November 1983 the Stroh Brewery Company began receiving calls and letters from fools who believed that for every case of beer sold, the company donated a dollar to Jesse Jackson's presidential campaign. (See, it's so easy to start rumors because people are gullible enough to believe anything.) As a nice touch to this rumor it should be noted that it would have been illegal for them to donate money because a federal law prohibits corporations from donating to political campaigns. The company took out ads to correct the misimpression as threats of boycotts and angry missives poured in.[6]

Another interesting case concerned Church's Fried Chicken, which battled rumors in the '80s that the chain is run by the Ku Klux Klan and secretly spices its chicken with a chemical that sterilizes the black men who patronize the joints. (As if the KKK could mastermind a multi-city neighborhood depopulation conspiracy.) What's interesting about this rumor is how Church's business strategy *backfired* on them. The company's system was to buy up bargain stores in low-rent urban areas, allowing them to hit their targeted 21 percent return on capital. By doing this the stores seemed to be targeting black neighborhoods because they unintentionally were mostly ending up in black neighborhoods. Part two of the problem was this: have you ever seen a Church's Fried Chicken commercial on television? I haven't. With little or no advertising budget the franchise remained a mystery to many consumers. We trust chains like McDonald's and KFC partially because we see them on TV all the time and thus assume them to be reputable. Church's was an unknown, ripe to be ravished by rumor. The combination of these two factors and the ambiguously religious name set them up perfectly for suspicion.[7]

I would like to point out once again that all the above rumors are completely untrue, and the companies involved fought long and hard to disassociate their names from the misconduct alleged against them. I cite the rumors here to jog your creativity as you make up rampant rumors to circulate about your target company. A lot of those rumors have circulated again and again over many years, proving that what has provoked emotion in the past will certainly provoke it again, so take your pick and change the names and logos to reflect the company you want on the death block.

General Industry Rumors

Some stores rely on the good fortunes of a particular industry to stay in business, and when that industry suffers, so too the company or store. As an example publishers' profits are linked with the bookseller industry. I know of one publishing company that lost $20 million in sales because Waldenbooks was going down the tubes as Barnes & Noble expanded. These things cut across all forms of business. "Cutbacks in budget and personnel in corporations across America have affected us immensely," Hal Rosenbluth, CEO of a travel agency, wrote. He went on to say:

> We manage the travel accounts of nearly two thousand corporations, and when times are hard for them, we share the burden. When budgets are slashed in cost-cutting measures, travel is one of the first discretionary expenditures to be cut. And when our clients make the choice to reduce their travel programs, we can suffer huge losses because we have assumed the resources to provide service for their original volumes[8]...
>
> When corporations face economic hardships, when they're faced with slumps in their industry, they're forced to drastically cut expenses. This creates a shock wave up and down the food chain... No one escapes these troubles.[9]

For these reasons you may consider ways in which your target company might be affected by general industry rumors or other attacks as well as specific attacks on the company. This can be helpful if you're trying to get your story out by legitimate media, for instance, where they may be more likely to air your concerns if you don't mention a company by name. Every so often the media flares up with one horror story or another. We've seen the stories about apples poisoned by pesticides, cellular phones causing brain damage, and so on. Rumors of these sorts attack entire segments of business, rather than a specific product. The apple-pesticide story attacks all apple sellers as opposed to attacking one farm in particular. If a business is already shaky, the reduced business is just one more pin bursting their balloon.

Creating and Spreading Rumors

You'll want to create a rumor or rumors that are believable, simple to understand, and thus easy to pass on in a short conversation, e-mail, or fax.

If there's a name in the company name, use that against them: "You've heard of McGregor Motors. But have you heard of great-great-grandpapa McGregor's slave owning days…?"

If the corporate name is inscrutable (Arnat Industries) you can make up a derogatory phrase that fits. "Hey did you know how they chose that name? The founder was joking around about the toxic chemicals used in his production process: 'Acid Rain Not A Trouble.' Those bastards!" Rumors can be born from the images and logos which companies use to represent themselves. The Proctor & Gamble logo was easily twisted around to fit a deviant message. The cover of *McDonald's Treasure Land Adventure,* a video game put out by Sega Genesis and McDonald's, offers similar evil-twistability. The box shows an overjoyed Ronald McDonald (the ecstatic red-haired clown) swinging across a cable high above a river, clutching onto jewels and treasures, while the other McDonald's characters cheer him on. This image is meant to sell a trite video game, but can be twisted around to illustrate how McDonald's is a greedy corporation, clutching onto the money for dear life. Such an image could even be cut out and pasted into a newsletter, and shown out of context with appropriate comments would be the kind of thing to get folks thinking negatively of the company.

Use a reputable source in your rumor:

"A company executive admitted on *20/20* that…"

"A public-relations representative told Oprah that they…"

"A dissatisfied former vice president told a conservative radio talk show host…"

Even a seemingly "nice" rumor can have harmful consequences. Nike supposedly sends you a free pair of sneakers if you send them a used pair for recycling (the way their sales have been lately they may need to give away shoes). The rumor went around that Gerber Products was settling a class-action suit by giving away a $500 savings bond to every child born between 1985 and 1997 — a complete fabrication of course, but Gerber fielded over 18,000 phone calls in one month alone. The costs of lost productivity and extra staffing to answer stupid phone calls starts adding up.[10]

What's the best way to spread rumors? Tell people who are in a position to speak to lots of other people, such as cab drivers or beauticians. If you know any stand up comics or public speakers, encourage them to say nasty jokes or put down the company. Rumors often spread through anonymous fliers left here and there about town. The Proctor & Gamble rumor that had died down in the early 80s resurfaced again in 1985 when an anonymous one-page flier started circulating.[11] It's even easier nowadays to spread fliers what with personal computers, office copiers, fax machines, and e-mail. Zines offer another way of getting the word out. During World War II, a cigarette company paid two well-dressed men to spread rumors on New York subways during rush hour. In lively and loud tones, they discussed how a German submarine landed off the North Carolina coast, commandos disembarked, found one of the rival cigarette company's warehouses there — and started spraying it with poison gas. "Sure glad I don't smoke Brand X!" they'd say, and reportedly sales of Brand X fell sharply during the negative campaign.[12]

Results of Rumors

It's sometimes said that even bad publicity is better than no publicity at all because it gets your name out there. The idea is that later on people will remember your name, not remember the bad things associated with it. Like when a TV reviewer runs a clip from a film, explained Jeffrey Godsick, "Executive Vice President of entertainment at Rogers & Cowan, the largest publicity agency in Hollywood" (well lah dee dah, I'm *soooooooo* impressed) in a *Harper's* roundtable discussion, "If the clip works with our advertising position, then they're supporting our campaign, even if they give us a bad review."

"And we only give them clips that support our message," punched in Mark Gill, the senior V.P. of this and that for Columbia Pictures.[13] See, those big shots wearing Armani the way reptiles sport scales, hardly give a hoot at all about bad reviews (bad publicity). It's only the positioning that matters. (Consider all the awful horror movies, kung fu capers, stupid comedies, and other cinematic disasters inflicted upon us each year. They get bad reviews out the wazoo, but still make money because teenage boys go see them. It's the positioning that counts — so attack their positioning.)

On the other hand... I can't help but feel that those movie executives don't know squat (consider aforementioned horror movies, kung fu capers, stupid comedies, etc. How could they know anything and still make those movies? And I haven't even gotten into romantic comedies staring unfunny sitcom stars). It's hard to believe wholeheartedly that bad publicity is just as fine as good publicity. Consider the Tylenol case. In 1982 someone inserted cyanide into Tylenol capsules, killing seven people. Through no fault of their own, Johnson & Johnson was faced with an incredibly damaging and costly situation (about $100 million dollars), withdrawing all the bottles from the shelves, suffering incalculable injuries to the Tylenol brand name, and feeling bruised and battered by a financial community that thought they were crazy to spend that much just to withdraw the product from the shelves. It was such a widely covered news story that within a week it was estimated that more than 90 percent of the American public were aware of the situation (and you know how out-of-it at least 50 percent of the American public is). No one wanted to go anywhere near Tylenol. They couldn't trust it. Now years later if you mention Tylenol to anyone, people can tell you all about the Tylenol poisoning incident, but long forgotten are the Sudafed poisoning incident, or any of the myriad other tamperings that have come up from time to time. Extremely bad news does live on in the public consciousness.

Finally, if you can motivate people to take action against the company because of the bad news, they will certainly remember the company in a bad light. That's where things like rumors come in — people remember boycotting Ford, Pepsi, or Volkswagen for being allegedly anti-Semitic companies. They remember writing a complaint letter to a CEO. They remember when they were so outraged that they stopped patronizing a store or business. You might even be able to motivate people to act on their own inner sense of evil. After the Tylenol poisoning incidents, a man was convicted of attempting to extort $1 million dollars from Johnson & Johnson, apparently in order to prevent him from poisoning again. That man was arrested. But there may be instances, if handled correctly, where the company feels threatened, has an image to uphold, secrets to keep, or they don't wish to turn to the police. In the spirit of corporate wastefulness, they pay the extortionist. And then you've really got a story you can badmouth them with in the media!

Learn More

■ **www.urbanlegends.com**

■ **urbanlegends.miningco.com** These are two sites devoted to urban legends (rumors). Use them for further information and ideas on creating rumors of your own on the business you seek to hurt.

■ **www.snopes.com** Another urban legends page, this one run by the San Fernando Valley Folklore Society, to help stimulate your thinking in scandalous ways.

📖 *Factsheet Five.* P.O. Box 170099, San Francisco, CA 94117. Sample issue $5; Canadian orders $6; European orders $8; Asian/Pacific Rim orders $9. This magazine is an ever-changing museum of zines of all stripes, to which you can submit zines to be reviewed. Say you develop a nice-looking flyer about the company, how they ripped you off and others, why people should boycott them, and offering tips on preventing the company's long-term survival. Start distributing your zine to those who can help, and send one in to the editor. If *FS5* reviews your zine favorably (or at all), you're sure to receive a number of requests for copies, thus helping to spread your word all across this great land of ours.

Attack #2. Phone Fun

Companies spend a lot of money on their telephone systems, so anything you can do to waste that money is a sure boon to your cause. Most toll-free numbers are listed in the AT&T directories, or sometimes they are on the front window of the store.

- **Tie up their toll-free line.** Every second you spend on their toll free 800 or 888 line is money they're wasting. Call from pay phones and ask ridiculous questions. Ask legitimate questions. Ask anything! Especially call during lunch hour and other busy times. Your goal is to make sure legitimate paying customers can't get through. This trick was worked against the Reverend Jerry Falwell in 1986.[14] Gay newspapers advised their readers to call Falwell's 800 line in opposition to Falwell's stance on homosexuality. The line was ostensibly for viewers requesting information on Falwell's television show, and to donate money to Falwell's cause. The gay activists tied up Falwell's lines so badly that contributors could not get through to donate money! One guy set up his computer to dial the number every 30 seconds. Falwell was eventually forced to shut down his toll free line and lay off 225 staff members after the telephone attack.

- **Bogus orders.** If possible place a lot of C.O.D. and "bill later" orders to phony addresses.

- **Infuriate company representatives.** They will become all riled up and may treat the next legitimate customer harshly, which can't be good for business. Another trick is to try and get a manager or supervisor on the line. Managers are paid more than the pantheon of customer service reps, so theoretically if they're stuck on the phone talking to you, the company will be wasting even more money.

- **Slow down their BBS or web page.** Many computer companies have web pages or electronic bulletin board systems that you can call up, download upgrades, and obtain information. Get together a group of computer nuts to log in at peak times so legit customers will become frustrated as they can't get through.

- **Use up their voice mail.** Leave long messages on their voice mail. The goal is to completely fill up their voice mail boxes so real customers can't phone in their orders and concerns. You especially want to target salespeople and customer service reps.

- **The answering machine.** Smaller companies might not have voice mail, but they will have one or more answering machines. Sometimes one crucial answering machine services an entire company! If you can fill it up with garbage, then no legitimate sales or customers can get through. This is especially damaging over a long weekend.

- **A direct connection.** Get the direct phone number for the company president and other higher-ups from the company directory. Scribble them on public bathroom walls ("Suzy gives good sucky!") and publicize them as phone sex lines.

- **Complain, Man!** Call their customer service line and complain about specific employees, complain about company practices, and complain about anything you can think of to complain about.

It is best to try these tactics right when a big ad campaign is unleashed. That way anyone who really wants to buy their products can't get through, and eventually they'll give up and go to a competitor. All the money spent on the ad will have been in vain. Another tactic is to pair this kind of attack with a reputation attack. PepsiCo experienced this unfortunate double-whammy in November of 1996, when they experienced problems with their telephone service during a time the media was broadcasting scare messages about the link between aspartame and brain tumors.[*] Concerned callers could not get through to hear reassuring words and facts from Pepsi's perspective. Also, because of their technical troubles, Pepsi was forced to temporarily switch to another phone carrier that offered less interactive features, making Pepsi look a little cheap for not offering those features. This was also bad for the phone company because they lost business, and lost the respect and confidence of PepsiCo.

Attack #3. Boycott Their Profits

Find out what products or services are most profitable for the business, and then arrange a boycott against them. Make sure the boycott is one that will stick in people's minds long after it has ended. Years from now people should still harbor a bad feeling about the company, even when the boycott has (unfortunately) ended.

You're in luck if your company's in the perishable foods business. That's what happened when customers tried to break a banana price cartel in 1975. They let the bananas rot on the dock, and the cartel was dismantled a year later.[15] Foods are also susceptible to tampering, injections of poison, or shards of glass mixed in them. Food companies have suffered millions of dollars of expenses when even threats of such actions have been made. In worst-case scenarios the company is forced to recall packages off store shelves which must be examined and destroyed; they find themselves flooded with

---

[*] Pepsi's telephone problems were technical in nature, and not caused by someone intentionally trying to undermine them.

negative publicity, and consumers sensibly enough refuse to buy the product. You can also elicit help from stores in this manner. When glass was found in jars of baby food, signs started appearing in store windows: "For your protection, we suggest that you not buy Gerber baby food until further notice."[16]

One boycott that worked for a little while was the one against popcorn sales in movie theaters.[17] Theaters make most of their profits from food and drinks, not from the showing of movies! (A large cup of soda can cost them about 5 cents for the cup, 7 cents for a squirt of cola-flavored syrup, and a few more pennies for the carbonated water. If they charge $3 for a large soda, about $2.80 of that is pure profit! That's why they won't give out the cups for free.) Some sources have estimated 70% of theater profits are due to the concession stand sales. Thus you can imagine how pissed theater owners were when people started boycotting popcorn. The public became aware that the popcorn — often thought of as a light, airy, healthy snack — was being popped in coconut oil which contains more fat than a handful of lard! People started boycotting popcorn and sales took a quick nose-dive. Unfortunately, the theater owners switched to canola oil which patrons perceived as healthier, and sales eventually turned up again for them. Canola oil, like any kind of fat, isn't really a great thing to eat a lot of, but people were desperate to munch on something during the movies. In *your* boycott you will want to leave them with no way out, no way for the boycott to ever really end. For instance, if the theaters were your target, you wouldn't just boycott against coconut-popped popcorn, because all they have to do is switch oil, and the boycott will fizzle out. **Better:** Boycott the whole notion of buying anything at all from the concession stands. You could encourage people to take in their own food with them (most ushers and ticket takers don't care). Or you could sell cheaper snack food outside the theater.

As you continue researching the company you will undoubtedly find out something-or-other that can be used as the basis for a boycott. Every person, place, or thing has some terrible secret lurking in their past. For instance, did you know that Cadillac used to have a policy against selling cars to blacks? When they realized blacks liked buying the cars, they specifically started targeting their marketing to blacks[18] because greed beats discrimination any day. So pick up your trowel, keep digging up dirt, then boycott, boycott, boycott!

Spread the Word!

Spread the word about that evil corporation! These magazines and newsletters will help you publicize your cause.

📖 *The Animals' Agenda: Helping People Help Animals.* This magazine targets the animal-rights crowd. They have articles and news bits on companies which mistreat animals. Does your evil company harm animals in any way? Let them know about it! *The Animals' Agenda* is published by The Animal Rights Network Inc., 1301 S. Baylis St., Suite 325, Baltimore, MD 21224, (410) 675-4566. For editorial and advertising inquiries, contact them at: P.O. Box 25881, Baltimore, MD 21224

Here are some more of these kinds of newsletters:

📖 *Boycott Action News.* 1612 K St. NW #600, Washington, DC 20006. (202) 872-5307. E-mail: zorca@iia.org

📖 *Boycott Quarterly.* Center for Economic Democracy, Box 30727, Seattle, WA 98103-0127. E-mail: boycottguy@aol.com.

📖 *Bunny Huggers' Gazette.* P.O. Box 601, Temple, TX 76503

Attack #4. Get the Weirdos on Your Side

For some reason, all the biggest weirdos in the world seem to have most of the money, and a whole lot of paranoia to go with it. Whether you're talking about Scientology, the Christian Coalition, or other cults and religious fanatics, they've got plenty of dough and plenty of time on their hands. If you can get *them* against your target company, trust me, they will do everything in their power to run the company into hell.

- **Letters.** Send letters to large Christian Right groups charging the business with supporting gay rights, "non-Christian" values, or whatever the hot topic of concern is at the moment. Give specific examples of how the company advertises with offensive shows, sells disgusting materials, or is run by executives who have personally committed acts offensive to God. Sign the letter with a clergyman's name, and use appropriate letterhead, to lend clout.

- **Web Woes.** Get on the Internet and use your favorite search engine to come up with all the relevant Web sites for all the different religious groups. Then send e-mail to each, explaining how the company is against each of them. Of course all of your e-mails are complete fabrications, but they don't have to know that.

- **Advertise.** If you've got the bucks, put a prominent display ad in the *New York Times* or some other big newspaper, boldly proclaiming that Company X condemns this or that religious group. I guarantee that company will be immediately besieged by irate phone calls, graffiti artists, Molotov cocktails, and multiple painful boycotts.

Spread the Word!

📖 The reference department of any library will have several valuable resources to help you locate organizations and religious groups that you may want to send letters to. *Directory of Religious Organizations in the United States* by Gale Research gives addresses, phone numbers, descriptions, and number of staff, of many different kinds of religious organizations. Similarly the *Official Catholic Directory* published annually lists names and addresses of Catholic groups all over. The *Encyclopedia of Associations* comes in several volumes, which lists names, addresses, and descriptions of every association, organization, and club covering every topic people in their diversity could ever dream up.

▪ **www.blackbusiness.com** Use their directory to find out if your target company is black-owned. If so, I'm sure the KKK and other hate groups would like to know about it.

- **The Personal Touch.** Persuade your friendly neighborhood psychopath to turn his or her violent tendencies towards furthering your cause. That's what happened when a hired gun was sent out to protect the interests of a surgical corporation that was being attacked by animal rights activists. The hired gun focused on one activist in particular, a woman who was somewhat possessed to begin with. They pumped up the activist and directed her anger against the company president, planted ideas in her head about killing the president, helped her concoct a murder scenario, and finally bought her some bombs with which to do the job. They buttered her up with money, shows of wealth, pretend friendship, and psychopathic ideas. In the end they clued in the police department about the activist's resolve to kill the president, and a public arrest was made in order to show the world what nut cases the activists were.[19] Without that final action, who knows how far she would've gone in her plans.

■**┓**■**┓**■**┓**■**┓**■**┓**■

Attack #5. Pit Other Companies Against Them

Think about how you can induce other businesses to become a burden on the company. For example, every two weeks the Shell gas station near my home is bothered by people from the local law center asking for directions. What if you distributed flyers with directions to some nearby event, but wrote intentionally poor directions which forced people to stop into the target business, asking them for directions? Even better, distribute the flyers to people who have no interest in your target company at all.

Playing with innocent people can be fun. How about making the company's neighbors angry at the business? Order a ton of food from the next-door Chinese food place and have it delivered to the business. When neighbors hate each other, angers seethe and fists start fuming. It's said that:

> At lunch in the summer, Alfred Knopf, the publisher, liked to take iced coffee with his meals. When he moved his company to its current location on the east side of Manhattan, he thought he would try out the French restaurant across the street. The owner, a man named Fayet, refused to serve Knopf his iced

coffee. From then on, no one from Knopf's firm ate at Fayet's. That was a lot of expense-account lunching that went elsewhere. Fayet is no longer in business in New York.[20]

Did Knopf's wrath put Fayet out of business? Maybe, maybe not. But certainly having one more neighbor rallying for his success would have only helped keep the restaurant flourishing.

Some companies live a life of natural symbiosis with another firm, like the companies which clean apartments at Fort Bragg Army base, and the company which inspects those apartments. One cleans, the other inspects. Trouble is, say the cleaners, the inspectors are trying to run them out of business by repeatedly failing them. When an apartment fails inspection, it must be cleaned again, which costs time and money, and sometimes fines are levied for various reasons. Sometimes a cleaning company is removed from the "approved list" if they fail enough inspections. The cleaners were complaining that the new private inspections company was trying to put them out of business by making inspections unreasonably ultra-tough to pass.[21] So even if it's not possible to infiltrate your target company as an inside accomplice, it may be possible to find another business in which you can become a tough-assed "inspector." In many cases the customer becomes that inspector — returning products, asking for special discounts or privileges, and giving the staff a rough time. It adds to the bottom line.

Some companies have formed alliances and partnerships with other companies in order to gain an insider's look into the other company. Maybe you can convince another business in the same industry to team up with your target company; or if you have your own company you might find some way of teaming up with them yourself. Be sure to look both ways before crossing this street, however, otherwise your own company's secrets will smack into an oncoming spy. Other times companies team up against a common rival. It was rumored that IBM and Microsoft teamed up to "derail Apple Computer Corp. forever," in the words of John C. Dvorak, a popular computer columnist and guru.[22] (Let's tread carefully here, for one never knows how accurate the musings of columnists are...) The soap opera according to Dvorak goes as follows: Apple put in three years of research and development, and one million lines of programming code into a new operating system called Pink. Apple was also busy suing Microsoft for copyright infringements, which pissed off Microsoft to no end. Besides, Apple was a gnat in Microsoft's ass, an impediment to future growth, and a company that needed to be hurt. Especially troublesome might be this new system Apple was working on. Microsoft's PR firm rolled out a campaign which included "a dubious 'secret' memo" from Bill Gates in which Gates ranted about the poor relationship between Microsoft and Apple. So if Microsoft's no friend of Apple, maybe IBM (who had secretly been trying to buy Apple) can use that as an opening to get into bed with Apple. So IBM enters the picture.

IBM teamed up with Apple on Pink, forming a company called Tallgent, which was supposed to use the technology to improve both styles of computers for the good. From the start it was said that IBM treated the joint venture as a joke, changing their minds constantly, refusing to agree on key points, and in general acting as a roadblock to progress. In a sense they were negating Apple's three previous years' worth of work, and eventually the whole thing crashed and folded under the wing of IBM. Dvorak's idea is that this joint venture in which IBM caused the system to crash was a massive scam by IBM and Microsoft to shut down Apple, or at least shut down this project of theirs. How accurate is this chain of events? I'm sure all the parties would deny it vehemently. Perhaps it will give you some thoughts on how your company can team up and bite off the ear of the company you want to see go down.

Attack #6. Tree-Spiking Tactics

Tree-spiking is a tactic adopted by environmentalists combating the unfortunate problem of corporations chopping down ancient forests. They hammer spikes deep within trees in the forest. The spikes have the potential to damage tree-chopping equipment and even injure loggers. The company is warned that their forest has been spiked, sometimes spiked *years* in advance, to allow time for the spikes to become completely grown over with wood and bark. Once a forest becomes tainted by the threat or rumor of spikes, it becomes unwanted territory, for it's expensive to search for and remove the spikes, but it can be even more costly, and even deadly, to leave the spikes in.

Now, your target company may not specifically be destroying old growth forests, but there are lessons to be learned from the way environmentalists handle these sorts of problems, with tree-spikings, and similar monkeywrenching tactics. "When outnumbered and outgunned, you look for your opponent's weak spot, the place where he does not want to be hit. For corporate America, that is generally the pocketbook,"[23] wrote

David Foreman. Foreman is a cofounder of Earth First! and has written extensively on monkeywrenching. Looking for the weak spot means finding what can be done to undo a deal, prevent business transactions, or derail a sale.

Any business that's building new sites or expanding can be a victim of monkeywrenching attacks. Foreman mentions some brilliant techniques: decommissioning heavy equipment, pulling up survey stakes, pouring sand in the crankcases of bulldozers, rendering dirt roads in remote areas inaccessible to vehicles, and cutting down billboards, to name a few.[24] In 1985 a group of "ecoteurs" firebombed a $250,000 chipper that was making mincemeat of a Hawaiian rain forest for power-plant fuel — bankrupting the operation.[25]

"Every available tool needs to be employed; every style, from business suits and laptops to camouflage and tree-spikes, needs to be encouraged,"[26] Foreman says. In a sense, this form of putting companies out of business is a way of standing in for the trees and animals who can not defend themselves against the onslaught of modern corporate expansion.

Ecologists and animal lovers have for years strived to put whole industries out of business using these sorts of tactics. A typical report is the one that happened the summer of 1997, when "ecoterrorists" released thousands of minks from a farm near Mount Angel, Oregon, near Portland. The minks ran wild, and many died of exposure, trampled each other, or killed one another in fights. Many of the minks that died were babies. When presented in the media, these facts do not exactly make the animal-rights activists look good. The most costly previous attack, said a spokesperson for the Fur Commission U.S.A., was a pipe bomb explosion in Utah.[27] It sounds like the damage-to-good-press ratio was fairly high there. Naturally you'll fare better because you'll think ahead about stuff like this. To do a really good job, you'll want to make sure that you or your group looks good in the media too so you derive full benefit from the stunt.

Don't just destroy randomly because it's fun. Be sure what you're destroying will have the effect intended, Foreman cautions: "Monkeywrenchers know that they do not stop a specific logging sale by destroying [just] any piece of logging equipment they come across. They make sure it belongs to the proper culprit. They ask themselves what is the most vulnerable point of a wilderness destroying project, and strike there. Senseless vandalism leads to loss of popular sympathy."[28]

Think all this is wrong? Undemocratic some would argue, as it imposes a few extremist beliefs on others. Well foo foo to you. Foreman responds to that argument with zeal: "This ignores evidence that our system is far from democratic — owing to the excessive power wielded by wealthy corporations to influence politicians through campaign donations and outright bribes, and through their advertising dollars in the media."[29] And let us all say *amen.*

Attack #7. Mail Tricks

You can impede the company using these malicious mail tricks:

- **Change of address forms.** Go down to the post office and fill out a "Change of Address" card for the business and key executives. Have the post office deliver all their mail *to their arch rivals.*

- **Embarrassing subscriptions.** Sign up the big bosses to magazines and send away for embarrassing junk mail that keeps coming and they have to deal with. All magazines are good, but especially pornography or potentially embarrassing magazines are best. If you're trying to take down a Dude Ranch, you would subscribe the company president to a vegan magazine. Eventually the bill will come, and they will either pay it, wasting money, or they will receive threatening letters for a long time to come. Make sure you tip the media about that president's incongruous inclinations.

- **Sign up the competition.** Make sure the company's arch rivals receive every mailing the company sends out. Every time the company sends out a press release, catalog, update, or newsletter, you should get them to mail copies to the executives of competing companies in their field. It shouldn't be hard to call or write to your company, request information, and give them the names and addresses of the competition. If the competition is smart they will make good use of this information when planning their own promotional campaigns.

- **Remove them from competitors' mailing lists.** On the other hand, if your target company receives mailings from its competitors, they could use the information to their advantage. Therefore you want to try and remove them from those mailing lists. Call, fax, or write to competing companies, making special requests to remove their names from their mailing lists.

Some people take these things to the extreme. *Forbes* reported the story of Reynaldo Fong who wanted to get revenge on a lawyer after losing a bidding war. For the next ten years he signed her up for *almost* 100,000 magazine subscriptions, billing them to her, of course. He also sent her a refrigerator — C.O.D. The lawyer whined it cost her $50,000 to straighten out the mess. Well, Fong has a year in prison now to think about the mess he made for himself, and after that he gets deported.[30] And after that, who knows? Maybe by then he'll be pissed off enough to raise the figure to well *over* 100,000 — and sending from a foreign country maybe he won't get caught this time.

Attack #8. False Advertising

Advertising is supposed to help a company, but it can also hurt it if you're the one who makes up the advertising!

- Print up a bunch of fake coupons offering steep discounts. Watch the sparks fly as customers try to pass off the coupons to puzzled employees. Watch the inter-departmental cat fights as employees blame each other for a botched marketing attempt that no one wants to take credit for.

- Pass around phony fliers advertising something they can not supply and then report them for bait-and-switch tactics. (Distribute the fliers near law firms.)

- Take advantage of free ads whenever you can get them in local papers. Promise the impossible, and the company will have to either deliver, or look like liars denying the ads were placed.

Forging More Realistic Ads

Many of these ideas (fake advertising, coupons, memos, letters from the company) will look more realistic if you include the company's logo and trademarks on the letterhead or envelope. You can start by first writing a letter to the company telling how lousy their products are. Naturally they will write back a soothing letter to you, and now you will know exactly what their corporate letterhead and envelopes look like!

Forging a letterhead is an easy task in this age of computers: simply visit the company's web site. Nowadays almost all businesses have a web page, and certainly that web page includes the company's logos on it.

Here's how to capture graphics in web browsers. In Microsoft Internet Explorer for Windows, right-click on the logo graphic, then click on **Save Picture as**. You can then type a filename and select a directory on your computer where you wish to store the graphic. In Netscape 3.0 right-click on the graphic, then click on **Save Image As**. A SaveAs box will appear with the filename in place. Choose a directory and change the filename if desired, then press **Save**. That's the best way to capture a logo, since you're getting it as a graphics file straight from the source.

If you can't do that for some reason, another method is to use a scanner to scan the logos into your computer off some literature you get from the company. Once you have the graphic saved, it is easy to insert it into your word processing document. That will give your fakes a more realistic look.

- Put up ads in the supermarket and on community bulletin boards saying you're looking to sell your boat, offer tutoring, or baby-sit children. Put down important company phone numbers, or even cell phone numbers that the company will be unhappy are being misused in this way.

- Send an invoice to the company "for the ad they placed in the yellow pages." To make it realistic, include a photocopy from a legitimate yellow pages ad they've placed, as a way of showing them what their ad looks like all printed up in your fictitious phone directory. Maybe they'll buy into it and send you a check to pay for the phony ad they did not place.

Attack #9. Media Maneuvers

There are tons of TV news programs always on the lookout for a company to clobber. Shows like *Hard Copy,* CNBC's *Steals and Deals,* and news segments like *Shame On You* love putting big ol' nasty mega-corporations on the spot. At the end of every news show is a hotline number you can call to report a potential news story. If you've got a legitimate gripe about the company, perhaps you can get your story told on the air.

Some newspapers have a consumer complaint columnist whom you might persuade to give your company some negative exposure. Chuck Whitlock, who investigates scams and frauds for various news programs, said that when he solicited scams using an 800 number, he "quickly discovered that a number of people who'd reported scams to us were attempting to scam *us* by making false allegations... these callers had a vendetta and were looking for a way to ruin someone's reputation."[31] So if you're going to make up false allegations about the company, better make up a hell of a lot of false proof and eyewitness testimony to back up your claims.

Radio talk shows can be another means of getting your message across. Think of a way your grudge or grievance can be related to the show's theme, then call the show and mention coyly that you know of a company who _____ (whatever — fit it to the topic, and make the company look really bad).

(You have to be truthful here, otherwise you're liable to be sued for slander, or defamation, or both.)

If a representative from the company appears on a show, contact the show and explain that you'd like to deliver the opposing point of view, to be fair to the viewers (you claim in that righteous All American tone of yours). Promote yourself as sane, telegenic, and likable — but also filled with short interesting anecdotes that the audience will eat up, yum yum. Then go on and blast away.

Companies take bad media exposure seriously. AT&T faced this problem in the summer of 1994. A toll-free phone number was set up in Northern California by a group called Prevent Handgun Violence Against Kids Public Education Campaign. PHVAKPEC (catchy acronym, yeh?) put up this free phone line with a pro-gun control message recorded by Ed Asner, that was preceded by the statement: "This call is being monitored by AT&T 800 Security." (AT&T has a service available to customers in which they monitor and provide security for potential abuse on 800 lines. They check on crank calls at the request of customer.) But unfortunately for AT&T, the statement "This call is being monitored by AT&T 800 Security" sounds a tad Big Brotherish, and it became a conversation point on KPAY-AM 1060 radio in Chico, California. Callers started ranting and raving furiously about why a telephone company would monitor calls, sponsor such a biased message, or take a position on gun control in the first place. This little incident was growing and growing until talk started that Rush Limbaugh might be considering the controversy as a topic for his program.

Boy oh boy, don't you wish that your target company faced such harsh media exposure as this? A smaller company might have crumbled under the pressure. AT&T is a big enough boy he can take care of himself. They brought out its senior legal advisor and other assorted big shots, called a big meeting with plenty of doughnuts and coffee, and spoke with the PHVAK-PEC people and Interstate Telemarketing (the service bureau that had set up the phone line message), and they insisted that PHVAKPEC remove the statement from the 800 line. PHVAKPEC did remove the message, and AT&T contacted the radio station and talk show host to correct the misimpressions. And that's called damage control.

Lesson: The media is a beast that needs to be fed, and many media outlets have discovered that the billions of people who make up the American public are great chefs. We come up with the most fascinating stories on all topics, and they'll print your story, let you say it on the air, and repeat it indefinitely, all in the name of putting content out there for the home audience. Even if it ain't exactly true.

Here are some more ideas:

- Perhaps there is a way to bring the tabloids into your ball court. One farmer in North Dakota was shocked by all the attention he received when the *World Weekly News* reported a story that his field contained a stinking hole to hell, littered with bones. The town and farm quickly became overrun with curious folk who wanted to see hell for themselves.[32] Maybe you can come up with some sort of variation on this so as to make your target company's life hell.

- Announce to the media that their product is being recalled due to scary, dangerous defects.

- Whistleblow. Speak up about disgusting or unethical practices perpetrated by the company.

- Use the results of opinion polls cr surveys in your announcement. Naturally you don't want to waste time actually conducting a poll, so just make up the figures to suit your needs. The media never checks anyway. (On the other hand, if you do take a poll it might be a good way to get in contact with people who share your negative opinion of the company and thus with whom you might team up against the company.)

- Suppose the company president's name is Ross Williams. You call up the newspaper to report a mistake in yesterday's Crime Beat column. You tell the paper you are Police Chief Grimsby and they mistakenly reported Saul Jones as the guy who was arrested for marijuana possession. Lambaste the paper! Say "How dare you! Saul is the *lawyer* — he'll sue you! The guy arrested was *Ross Williams!*"

That's Step #1. Step #2 is to use the "correction" against the company. Make sure people know Ross Williams was arrested for drugs. A surprising number of people see these little things in the paper anyway, and even more will when you start clipping and saving and distributing all these tidbits that you've planted here and there through the media. And remember the words of Philip Leslie, when asked by a *Wall Street Journal* reporter why he was coming to the media about his desire to see the company he founded go out of business after being taken over by outsiders: Because, he said, the media offers just one more opportunity "to try to pound the daylights out of those guys."[33]

📖 *How YOU Can Manipulate the Media: Guerrilla methods to get your story covered by TV, radio, and newspapers* by David Alexander. Paladin Press. Boulder, Colorado. 1993. Lots of interesting advice and anecdotes on how others have successfully gotten their point across on the air.

Attack #10. Start an Anti-Corporation Web Page

The World Wide Web provides a fantastic way to get a message across to millions of people worldwide. Many consumers have started web pages to attack companies after being poorly treated by them. Feeling no other recourse they put up a page on the Net explaining the horror story the company put them through, and how the company responded inadequately to their complaints.[34] When Jeremy Cooperstock put up a page blasting United Airlines, it received 1,500 hits (people visiting the page) over a three-month period. Two hundred and twenty seven of those visitors were logging in from United computers. Maltreated customers have put up sites roasting every company from Infiniti cars, Nike, Mitsubishi, Guess jeans, and more.

Creating a web page is as easy as typing up a document in a word processor. You can go to the store and buy web page design software, or if you're not too computer savvy, you're sure to meet up with someone who is as you gather team members to help fight the company. You then need to find an Internet service provider who can host your page. In other words, you need to find a company that has computers connected to the Internet. They help you copy your web page onto their computers, making it accessible to every connected soul in the whole world. Many Internet service providers help you create your web page, too.

It may be tempting to use corporate logos on your web page (usually with the word "SUCKS!" emblazoned underneath), but you open yourself to legal action if you try it. Web pages are *not* anonymous unless you take great pains to make them so.

You're going to have to work hard to get a lot of people to visit your site, and if you're talking about a no-name corporation you may have to work even harder to get people to visit. There are two ways for people to access (hit) your site:

A.) People can type in your address and go directly there.

B.) Or they can link there from another site.

If you do a lot of advertising, publicity, press releases (Attacks #8 and #9 above) then you've got A covered. But the bulk of the visits should come from B. You want people to link to your site from other places. That means you have to get your site listed in all the search engines and on-line listings, and people have to be able to find it.

To really get a lot of hits, you want your site to win the position of "Featured Page of the Day" or "Web of the Week" on various pages. There are certain well-traveled pages that show off really good sites. Those featured sites get a lot of hits. So the first thing is to make your site a really good site (useful information, downloads, freebies). It might be helpful to present your site as a legitimate news source presenting astonishing news about the company, rather than the rantings of an angry consumer. If you sponsor a contest with a fabulous prize then you'll get tons of people flooding your site. Once you've got an incredible site, start submitting it to the different pages and they will see how wonderful it is and feature your page on their page. It's especially good if you can get yourself placed on the Netscape page or the Microsoft page, something like that. To further encourage visitors, do the following:

- Provide useful information instead of just ranting and raving. If you have useful information it will be more likely to get reviewed by the directories and search engines, and then more people will be able to find it. There is also another reason to provide information: As you put more key words on your page it will turn up more frequently in searches.

- Puts lots of cool stuff on the page: freebies to order, downloads, cool graphics, sound, and animation, to incite people to visit. You can hold contests, such as, "Describe why you hate Company X in 50 words or more..." This gets other people thinking *and acting* along the same lines as you.

- Make your page fast loading. Don't use more than two or three frames (if any). Don't have a huge corporate logo as the opening graphic. People are impatient and they don't like wasting money on their phone bill to load a slow site. They'll back out before it even loads. So make sure your site is speedy.

- Once you have a great site, start submitting it to magazines that review web sites. Some magazines are *Wired, Internet World, NetGuide*, and *Online Access*. You probably have some local computer newspaper they distribute in the food stores. Go to the office and use the photocopiers to make a million flyers that you can hang up everywhere. Do whatever it takes to get your site out in public view.

- Make a signature file that contains your web address and a brief description of what's there. Then start communicating with people on relevant mailing lists and newsgroups. People will start noticing your signature and ask you about it if they're interested.

- Cities and communities often have pages of their own (Philadelphia LibertyNet). Try to get listed in your local community's page.

- Another way to advertise is to spam newsgroups. This will anger a lot of people but if anyone's interested it will certainly get the word out. It's easy to spam newsgroups. Use whatever news reader software you normally use, type up an ad, and send it out to as many groups as you want. (Best if done from within the company's offices.)

- And of course do all the other off-line publicity, advertising, press releases, and all the rest of it that anyone does when publicizing a new business or opportunity.

- Finally, visit the web sites listed the next two pages and do everything there.

Getting people to visit your site is a matter of having a good, fast site, with stuff that people want to see and use, and giving people plenty of access to it. If you take this seriously and really do a lot of these things then a lot of people will have access to your site, and they will want to visit. That doesn't mean they will want to help you put the company out of business, but at least you might plant the thought in their heads that there is something wrong with that corporation.

- **misc.consumer** is a USENET newsgroup (Internet discussion forum) where you can complain about companies. There are tons of newsgroups on many topics, so you can post your complaints and damaging anecdotes to many newsgroups to gain broader exposure.

- **www.yahoo.com/Business_and_Economy/Consumer_Economy/ Consumer_Opinion/** is a nice organized list of links to all the pissed off folk out there trying to get back at companies. Check out those pages for ideas of your own (and possibly people to recruit).

- **www.2020tech.com/submit.html** The Internet Promotions Megalist. This is a great resource. It's a huge list of forms and robots that will automatically add your site to hundreds of lists, catalogs, search engines, and directories. Just do everything on this page and you will be listed all over the place.

- **ep.com/faq/webannounce.html** This site describes how you go about announcing your new web site to the web community. It provides great info and appropriate links.

- **www.samizdat.com/public.html** How to publicize a new web site over the Internet.

- **www.smartclicks.com** Advertise your site for free in banners. There must be some catch, but it's worth a look.

- **www.yahoo.com/Computers_and_Internet/Internet/World _Wide_Web/Announcement_Services/Banner_Exchanges/** A huge listing of (mostly) free banner exchange networks. They put your banner on their sites, and in exchange you put their banners on yours.

- **www.yahoo.com/Computers_and_Internet/Internet/ World_Wide_Web/Searching_the_Web/Indices_to_Web_Do cuments/Free_for_All_Pages/** Huge list of graffiti walls, pages that will link to your page, directories, yellow pages, and the like. Just go down the list visiting each site, and advertise yourself everyplace.

■ **www.activmedia.com/netdirs.html** Tells how to list your site in net directories. Good info and links for you to use.

■ **www.web-mkt.com** Market your web page to over 25 search engines.

■ **www.exposepromotions.com** Expose Professional Web Site Promotion is one of many businesses that help you promote a web page for a price ($75-$150). These businesses submit your site to search engines and help you design your page for maximum hits. Though you may not wish to spend the money to promote your site in this way, visiting such pages may give you ideas on how you can publicize your page on your own.

Attack #11. Spam the Masses

Everyone hates a spammer, and wouldn't everyone hate it if your company started spamming too? A spammer is someone who sends out thousands of e-mail messages, unasked for, and unannounced. Spam is unliked the same way junk mail is unliked, because it's annoying, useless clutter, and often appears shady, as if a con artist or huckster sent out the e-mail. Also spammers often resend the same message over and over again, repeatedly angering people trying to read their e-mail in peace.

Spammers use several different methods to collect e-mail addresses. Some go into the America Online member directory and collect e-mail addresses, or they monitor Internet chat sessions for usernames. Some do it manually, others write a program to collect the info automatically. You can also buy software that does this.

The spam you send should be a little over the top, the way a late-night infomercial promises miracles that are a little bit too sensational to be believed. Be sure to include plenty of company phone numbers, faxes, addresses, and e-mail addressed in your spam, so the recipients of this e-mail will have plenty of means of contacting the appropriate culprits and bawl them out for sending such annoying spam. You can use spams in different ways: As a plea to boycott the company, to spread the message about what that company does wrong, and what competitors do right, or as a way of positioning the company in a bad light.

Get as Good as They Give

There's another side to this coin. You can help company employees get on the receiving end of junk e-mails and spams. Net surfers often receive spam after posting messages to newsgroups. For instance if you post to financial or investing groups you tend to get junk e-mails for unsolicited financial opportunities, pyramid schemes, and the like, many of which are illegal or plain crazy. So if you have access to company computers and web browsers, take some time to post messages to these newsgroups using employee Internet accounts. Also be sure to visit and post on sex-related and other newsgroups, and who knows what'll end up in their e-mail box. While you're messing around on their computers, see if you can remove spam filters from their e-mail software. Some e-mail software has filters that serve to automatically delete undesired junk e-mails. Remove the filters, and all those annoying spams will get through to annoy them to pieces.

- 🖥 **www.emagnet.com/** is the Email Magnet — automatically extracts e-mail addresses from AOL, CompuServe, Web pages, search engines, etc., for $99.

- 🖥 **www.cit.cornell.edu/cit-pubs/email/protecting-lists.html** See this site for information on spamming mailing lists. Really this site is about how to stop spamming, but it gives enough info to teach you how to do it.

- 🖥 **www.bessling.com/bulkcd.htm** You can also buy the addresses outright on a CD-ROM. This has a typical offer, 10 million addresses for $399.

Attack #12. Report Them to the Proper Authorities

If you have some true-life horror stories to tell about the company, or an active imagination, there are many agencies to which you can report them. This will have several effects. Consumer complaints of negligence or fraud are often the basis of investigations by the law. Some agencies keep a public record of what complaints have been filed against a business, and that certainly can't help them win new business. There are specific agencies and organizations that concern themselves with everything from animal testing, age and sex discrimination, and consumer fraud. You'll also want to report all maltreatment the company imposes upon you to the applicable better business bureaus. Unions may also be a boon to your cause. Some agencies and organizations which may be helpful are listed below.[35]

- ▶ Defective products can be reported to the Consumer Product Safety Commission, 4330 Eastwest Highway, Bethesda, MD 20207, (800) 638-CPSC, **www.cpsc.gov** This is an independent Federal regulatory agency whose aim is to reduce deaths and injuries due to dangerous products. Consumers can file complaints about faulty or dangerous products here.

- The National Fraud Information Center, P.O. Box 65868, Washington, DC 20035, (800) 876-7060 or **www.fraud.org** helps consumers battle frauds relating to telemarketing, telephone solicitations, and Internet scams. Suspected frauds can be reported to them, and the reports are passed on to the appropriate law enforcement or government agencies.

- Bum cars can be reported to the Department of Transportation's National Highway Traffic Safety Administration. Department of Transportation, 400 Seventh Street SW, Washington, DC 20590, (202) 366-9550 **www.nhtsa.dot.gov** There are also ten regional offices around the country that serve their local areas.

- If the company does business through the mail, you may send written complaints to the Direct Marketing Association Mail Order Action Line, 6 East 43rd Street, New York, NY 10017. Also postal inspectors will be interested to hear about cases of postal fraud and abuse. The postal inspector (not the postmaster), should be in the phone book's government listing.

- The United States Consumer Gateway **www.consumer.gov** is like a corridor containing many doorways to numerous sources of federal information.

- The Environmental Protection Agency, 401 M Street SW, Washington, DC 20460, (202) 260-2090 **www.epa.gov**

EPA protects the health of humans and the natural environment.

🐾 The Federal Communications Commission, 1919 M Street NW, Washington, DC 20554, (202) 418-0200 or (888) 225-5322. **www.fcc.gov** FCC develops and implements polices relating to radio, television and other electronic broadcasting. There are many regional offices that handle investigative and enforcement work of the commission.

🐾 The Food and Drug Administration, (301) 443-1544 or (800) 532-4440, **www.fda.gov** scrutinizes just about anything that goes into or on our bodies, as well as radiation-emitting devices like microwave ovens. They also check up on the food and drugs for farm animals and pets. There is also a Food Safety and Inspection Service which frets over meat, poultry, and eggs, and the packaging and labeling of these goods.

🐾 Consumer World, **www.consumerworld.org**, has EVERYTHING on this site, or at least it seems that way. This site has links to an enormous number of consumer-related pages and organizations, lawyers, consumer-rights information, and you-name-it.

🐾 ConsumerLine, **www.ftc.gov/bcp/conline/conline.htm** is run by the Bureau of Consumer Protection's Office of Consumer and Business Education. It offers the full text of consumer publications on many subjects. The Federal Trade Commission takes legal action against companies involved in bait-and-switch and other fraudulent practices. They can also be reached at: FTC, Pennsylvania Avenue at Sixth Street NW, Washington, DC 20580, (202) 326-2222. Or you can simply visit **www.ftc.gov** which has listings of

BBBs, departments, and consumer protection offices around the country serving your local area.

🖳 **www.bbb.org/complaints/consumerform.html** The Better Business Bureau's department of complaints.

🖳 **www.bbbonline.org** This is the online home of the Better Business Bureau. If your business is certified by this online BBB you want to complain heavily about the misconduct they've shown as you've dealt with them.

☎ **(800) 664-4435** The Consumer Affairs National HELP-LINE is a central number run by the U.S. Office of Consumer Affairs (750 17th Street, N.W. Washington, D.C. 20006). Citizens can call for personal assistance with handling consumer complaints on all subjects. Call 10am-2pm EST Monday through Friday. More information available at: **gopher://marvel.loc.gov:70/00/federal/fedinfo/by-agency/executive/consumer/usoca.helpline**

▄▟▜▟▜▟▜▟▜▀

Attack #13. Start Your Own Competing Business

One way to force a company out of business is to start a business of your own that does the job better, faster, more efficiently, cheaper, or with a whole new twist that makes what the old company's selling look outdated. One CEO with this warrior's attitude is Mitchell Leibovitz of Pep Boys: "I don't believe in friendly competition," he says, "I want to put them out of business." "Them" means all his competitors. Leibovitz gleefully snaps photos of closed auto parts stores, every time one of his competitors goes down the toilet. He happily burns and buries baseball caps with their logos on them — and then videotapes the ritual to show to all his Pep Boys employees. Leibovitz's strategy is focusing his stores on one thing — cars — and stocking only high quality parts, and trying to stock parts for every car on the road, even if some of those cars are old. He also uses various techniques to keep prices down.[36]

Revenge, pure and simple, drove Rose Blumkin to start up a furniture store right across the street from her family's store. See, fifty years ago, Blumkin started Nebraska Furniture Mart, a $150-million-a-year store that she ran until her business was taken away from her by her grandsons. How did she respond? Well, why don't you listen for yourself to the fire and brimstone seething from this 96-year-old grandmother:

> I wish to live two more years and I'll show them who I am... I gave my life away for my family. I made them millionaires. I was chairman of the board and they took away my rights. They said I shouldn't be allowed to buy anything. No salesman should talk to me. So I got mad and I walked out.[37]

Yow! Rose stormed out, and opened Mrs. B's Warehouse across the street. A family feud ensued, as Rose used her extensive knowledge of the industry, and loyalty to her customers, to try and beat the boys into the ground.

"They are the elephant, I am the ant," she declared to win sympathy for her cause.

And according to Mrs. B, the elephants didn't take this lying down. They tried to sabotage her enterprise, she said, by warning all their suppliers that if they start doing business with her, they'd stop doing business with them.[38] That was in 1991, and Nebraska Furniture Mart is still in business in

Omaha, Nebraska, so I guess the grandmother didn't get her wish — too bad. But Mrs. B is still in business too, fighting hard and strong and long.

Greed apparently drove some key people at Cadence Design Systems to leave and start their own rival business called Avant![39] An investigation revealed that an Avant! founder spent his last days at Cadence copying top secret programming code which he was later to revamp and sell as his own software. A vice president and engineer both left Cadence within four months of each other. It is also alleged that before the engineer left he secretly e-mailed four files containing trade secrets about Cadence's software to an outside e-mail address. By using these stolen trade secrets and programming code, Avant! was able to bring a product to market ultra-fast, and without the research and development costs resulting from Cadence's years of effort.

Avant! officials were indicted and put to trial for their misdeeds. It seemed they were too cocky for their own good. They shouldn't have brought their stolen product to market as quickly as they did for it drew suspicion to themselves. In retaliation "Avant! claims that Cadence employees have shorted Avant! stock and spread negative rumors to drive it out of business."[40]

One More Story

An executive was moaning about the problems plaguing her former company which had just closed. Her former company produced public domain books, such as old poetry and novels, uncopyrighted stuff. High profit margin, for there's no author to snatch up royalties, no agent to negotiate with, no perks to pay, and essentially no advertising because those sort of books sell by themselves. But Barnes & Noble caught onto the idea. They came out with their own line of public domain classics. Of course theirs were cheaper because there was no middleman to deal with, they published them and sold them in their own stores. Worse — their books were *nicer* looking. "They shut us out by this monopolistic tactic of theirs," she said, "being both producer and distributor of the product."

Having a competing business may not be enough to drive a company out of business. But it can be a very good start, and a focus point to achieve the goal.

Come Fly With Me

Once your rival business is up and running you'll want to start stealing the best workers away from your target company. Steal their top talent, cream of the crop representatives, and anyone who has any insider knowledge of the company. Anyone, even down to the lowest rungs, might be valuable to you. For instance, a janitor might know the ins and outs of sneaking into the place, or how to disable the burglar alarm. While all employees are valuable assets that can hurt a company if lost, "in sales, where customers and revenue are on the line, the act is more sensitive," wrote one business writer. "Salespeople have access to trade secrets, pricing structures, delivery schedules, and marketing strategies. Any rep who moves to the competition can easily give away information that a company spent years cultivating — and provide a big boost to a rival's sales organization."[41] This was the prime goal of Frank ("I'm gonna be their worst nightmare") Pacetta.

Fired from Xerox under mysterious circumstances, Pacetta charged back with a vengeance. He took a job at a smaller rival, and now Pacetta makes it his business to beat Xerox, to make them pay for letting him go.

"It's a war with Xerox. A *war*. Understand?" he grills new candidates.

And the candidates he most cherishes recruiting are those from Xerox itself — luring away his rival's best people is his top priority, and the key, he feels to slamming Xerox into the ground. "Xerox will never be a great company again. Never. You know why? Because I won't let them."[42]

Attack #14. Dry Up Their Advertising Budget

Advertising is expensive to buy and hard to turn into profits, thereby making it doubly costly. One idea is to set up a scam where you represent yourself as the salesperson from a popular radio station or newspaper. Sell them air time or ad space. Take their money, and run. (Find one of those seedy check-cashing places in another city to cash the check. Automatic teller machines are usually not too picky about whom they accept checks from, but you'll want to hide your face from the camera, and certainly don't deposit it into your own account.) Or drop some clues their way that radio is a good buy, then hook them up with the shadiest radio ad seller in town. Ask around to find the shady characters in the ad business — couldn't be too difficult to find shady admen.

When the company releases a legitimate ad it's your duty to try and minimize the effects of that ad as much as possible. Ideally you would want to somehow get a glimpse of the ad before it hits the streets (later we'll talk about infiltrating the company; one of the best reasons for doing so is so you'll know their ad strategies ahead of time). If you cannot see the ad before it goes out keep these points in mind:

- Try to see the ad as soon as possible and begin thinking about how you or their rival company can better the offer or steal their thunder.

- If the ad appears in a free magazine or pamphlets freely distributed at a trade show or left out on countertops, or in newspaper boxes, then take all copies of it. Rip out the ads and destroy them.

- For TV ads the best you can do is shoot the president and hope the news coverage overrides commercials. The commercial will then be rescheduled for 3 o'clock in the morning. A more realistic goal is to minimize the after-effects of the ad. If it's just a product ad (teaching about the product) then there is not as much need to worry. But if it's a "sale ad" (an ad that talks about a particular sale) then minimize the number of people who go to the sale. For instance, there could be a "problem" with the store's parking lot so nobody can park there during the sale. Get together your tag team of business-busters and fill their parking lot with every car, truck, and motorized vehicle you can lay your hands on. Many customers will be too lazy to look for a parking space elsewhere and simply drive off. Or abandon a rusting hunk of junk right in front of the entrance so customers can't drive in. If you've got the tools, attack any potholes or loose parts of their drive-way ramp or lot, making the holes larger and more dangerous to drive over. The night before you could spill stinking rotting garbage all over, spray paint the lot white so the lines aren't visible, and throw glass and jagged metal fragments everywhere. If they call the police, that creates just one more car in the lot to scare away customers. And if you call the fire department (anonymously, and from a pay phone please), they'll have a whole fire truck blocking incoming traffic.

When Success Hurts

It should be pointed out that even good advertising can be used against a company. There have been plenty of companies who've let success put them out of business. The story is told[43] of Harvey Harris who sold personalized calendars, and sold them very well. He sold them so well in fact that orders began piling up — and up — and up. The equipment used to print the calendars started failing from overuse, so he had to invest in new equipment, but tens of thousands of orders were continuing to file in and remain unfulfilled. The orders he did fulfill didn't pay fast enough, or enough money, to pay for the replacement equipment he had to buy to keep up. Harris was like Sisyphus pushing the boulder up the mountain every day, except that Harris's boulder was pushing him backwards into the ground. And eventually he ended up flattened.

> **Lesson:** If you can't prevent or alter their ads, try to take steps to prevent the company from delivering the promises their ads make. Machines may be monkeywrenched, or orders made to vanish from mountainous stacks in in-boxes, or payments might be siphoned off into Never Never Land.

Attack #15. Vandalism

Vandalism is too crude a word. Let's call these White Elephant Attacks. You don't know about white elephants? Okay I'll trot out the old story. King of Siam generously gave the gift of rare white elephants to other kingdoms whom he wished to see destroyed. White elephants were sacred creatures, not allowed to do work, and so considered a fine and generous gift. Problem was, the other kingdoms now had these great big eating machines, costly to feed and care for, and yet which could not provide any useful service in return.[44] Vandalism is your gift of the white elephant to the company you wish to see destroyed. The company's lawn and their cars, and building, are all things very precious, very necessary to maintain and keep healthy, and yet which don't give back much value to the business. The more they have to care and feed and tend to them, the less they have to contribute to more necessary aspects of the business. And if they stop caring and tending for them, everyone will wonder why they let their white elephants die.

Vandalism of the company may be fun, but it should be done with a purpose in mind. As wonderful as it may be to throw cow blood all over the sparkling white front wall of a fur company, think of how much more effective it would be to throw the blood the day of the big multimillion dollar meeting between the fur company and Bloomingdales. You have to distinguish between fun and terrorism. *You want terrorism.*

There are revenge tactics and things you can do to drive them crazy, like steal the staples out of their staplers, that will slow down workflow and perhaps lessen morale, but keep in mind that sort of thing does little to drive the company out of business. All it does is give you a good laugh and alert them to the fact that they're being targeted. It's better to do something that has been thought out to disrupt some of their long-range goals. Especially do stuff that causes in-fighting to develop and won't make them suspect an outsider.

These techniques are also handy to use when the business is young. For instance, new businesses often have a period of time when they are paying rent on a new building as they renovate or remodel it, but since they don't have any customers during this time, they're not bringing in any money. An example is the restaurant which wasted $34,000 in rent before it opened over a year and a half later due to lengthy renovation work.[45] Before-the-opening is a particularly vulnerable time for the business, and with a little bit of prodding from you, can be even more so.

Old or new, here are some ideas:

- **Glue their doors shut, or squirt super glue in their locks.** But try to do it on a red letter day when the lockout will be most effective.

- **Bumper stickers.** Gather up the most repulsive slogans from the KKK or some similar organization and stick them everywhere — to employees' cars, store windows and walls, and to expensive merchandise.

- **Throw lots of jagged rocks and metal scraps all over their lawn.** The idea being to put their lawn mowers out of commission. Let them waste time and money repairing needlessly broken lawn mower blades. (If they're an agriculture company or a farm, there are plenty of ways of destroying fields of crops.)

- **Poison their lawn.** While you're at it, might as well spread detergent, bleach, salt or gasoline or some other poisonous substance all over their lawn (especially good a few days before the big stockholder's meeting, so everyone will be able to soak in the atmosphere of death). You can also spell out all sorts of nasty comments in the lawn. Try to make them visible from the road.

- **Deface company vehicles.**
- **Halloween pranks.** I'm sure on Halloween (or any day for that matter) you can convince some juvenile delinquents to ransack the place.
- **Threats.** Harassing phone calls and threats may incite the owner to throw in the towel.

Imagine if you could do all this to such an extent that the company is forced to close down or even move. That would be great! Think of all the many expenses that moving entails: phones, mail, stationery, business cards, and costs of moving. You might find out when their lease expires and see if you can put it into their heads that moving to another place might make their lives easier. Little do they know that trouble will follow them there as well.

Even short-term closures can have terrible consequences for a business. When an elevator support tower collapsed in Times Square, many area businesses were forced to close so tourists wouldn't get conked on the head by falling I-beams. The International Center of Photography Midtown was one of the places forced to shut down for three weeks. For almost a month the place shelled out salaries to employees who couldn't come to work, and of course tourists couldn't visit, so no money was coming in from admission fees or gift shop sales. The result — $20,000 in revenue lost forever; and even worse, for long afterwards customers stayed repelled from the area out of fear or ignorance because they didn't realize the doors had opened again. The center's director expected they'd probably never make back that money, "And if we do, it will take years."[46] Keep on your company's tail, stampede them with herds of white elephants long enough, and maybe you too can force a closure.

Attack #16. Attack Their Vehicles

Businesses need their trucks to deliver goods and services to customers. Salespeople need their cars to get to clients. All workers need their cars to drive to work and back. Wouldn't it be a shame if suddenly, all the workers at that company started having trouble getting to work in the morning, or they had trouble visiting clients, or delivering their products? Or if suddenly their cars were uglied up before going on a sales call, or before driving to someone's business dinner?

Larger businesses have security patrolling their parking lots — bad news for you. Lunchtime offers a reprieve. As workers head to the nearest fast food place in the middle of the day, look in their car in the restaurant lot. (Also you might be able to see whom are buddies if they go in a group, which might be helpful in your overall data-gathering on the firm.)

Many people feel safe in their office parking lots, and neglect to lock car doors, or they keep windows rolled down especially in summer months. Swipe cell phones, laptops, papers, briefcases, and other important goodies left in cars. Laptops are currently the hot new thing to steal and sell on the black market, so you've got to be careful. The company might have registered the laptops, or inscribed them with an authentication plaque that identifies it and can be used to ID it as stolen property. On the other hand, laptops are extremely valuable to corporations and will be surely missed. One New

York bank reported almost 100 laptops stolen over a two-year period, most of them from within the building.[47] The cost alone (100 × $2,500 = $250,000 or more) is a hurtful kick in the wallet, but the information on those laptops, if made available to the right people — or the wrong people — is incalculably costly to the organization.

Attack #17. Garbageology

Back in quaint olde 1955, Mr. Julius L. Sternitzky (retired inspector of the Oakland Police Department) was concerned with this very important method of corporate archaeology. Writing about his experiences on the police force, the inspector wrote that forgers would steal discarded papers from the trash and use the signatures on them to forge checks. "Many banks," he claimed "are now observing a warning given to them to remove checks and statements from wastebaskets which have been thrown into them after an error was made in writing the check or statement. The banks are especially watchful to see that no paper with signatures on it is left in the receptacles."[48] Of course you wouldn't stoop to forging checks, would you? Nah, you'd probably stick with credit cards and airline reservations.

Trash that company by poking around in their outside garbage dumps and bins. You'll find them useful in so many ways:

- **Industrial espionage.** You might find interesting tidbits that can work against the company: sales forecasts, marketing plans, internal memos, spreadsheets, or much more.

- **Embarrassment.** If your target is a medical facility, they might throw away confidential patient records, medical charts, or lab reports. Wouldn't it be embarrassing if some of that deeply private data got into the wrong hands? Wouldn't it be embarrassing if the local newspaper found out how lax this medical office is about its trash? Especially if some hypodermic needles and scalpels were found in the trash and distributed to neighborhood teenagers? Of course, the medical center didn't have to throw that stuff out. It might've been planted there by you, and somehow the word leaked out that this stuff could be found in their Dumpster.

- **Make a mess.** When you're done snooping, how about emptying out their Dumpsters and garbage cans, tossing around the garbage all over their lawn and property, and making a big mess. They'll be dealing with the mess for a while instead of more pressing matters.

  If you can break into the office you might have an easier time of sifting through trash cans and recycling bins. You might be able to get to important papers before they've made their way to the shredder. Some companies have locked security bins for shredding and recycling of confidential documents. These might be unlocked, or you might be able to pry them open. You can also trail the guy whose job it is to empty them and look for a weak link in the trail. Perhaps there's a time when he stops into someone's office to chat, leaving his rolling bin unguarded.

📖 *The Art and Science of Dumpster Diving* by John Hoffman. Loompanics Unlimited, Port Townsend, Washington, 1993. An interesting story on page 132 tells about Mrs. Spooner who ruined an organization by what she found in its garbage. "Another exciting thing I frequently find [in the trash] is information... for example, a list of fire safety violations at my least favorite local business. An anonymous letter here, a photocopy there, and next thing you know somebody's whole week is ruined."[49]

Attack #18. Take All They Offer

Take all the company has to offer. Exploit their generosity. They think that by being generous they will strike up a legion of loyal customers, but what they don't count on is you and your cohorts taking advantage of all that they offer (and there's no brand loyalty nowadays anyway).

- **Postcards.** Some companies put postage paid postcards in magazines. Make sure you send these in. Go to the library and rip out the postcards from magazines, so no legitimate customers can get their hands on them. Do the same at food stores, newsstands, and wherever they sell magazines. You can write nasty messages on the postcards and mail them, or an even better idea is to fill in fake names and addresses. That way the company will waste time and resources trying to mail information to bogus customers.

- **Free samples.** Take all the free samples they offer, especially if that means they have to mail it to you (postage is increasingly expensive). Depending on what kind of business it is, you might be able to use the sample against them. For instance, if it's a cookie company you can analyze the product and duplicate their recipe, then let everyone know what that recipe is. It also means possibly legit customers won't be getting as many free samples as you do.

- **Free refills.** If your target business is a restaurant, movie theater, or someplace else that offers free refills, an all-you-can-eat salad bar, or other freebie special, make sure you take special advantage of it. They count on customers being "nice" about the freebies, but there's no reason why you have to live up to their expectations.

- **Return policies.** Continuously make purchases then return the items, generating a lot of meaningless work for the company. If it's a mail-order shop make sure they pay the return postage too. (If it's a mail-order shop you might team up with your local credit card thief to place dozens of bogus orders and have them shipped to the other side of the country.)

- **Do-it-yourself.** They don't give anything away, you say? Well how about you help them give stuff away. Like, hire them for a project, don't pay, then disappear halfway through.

Later on in this book we'll talk about getting company insiders involved in your quest for corporate demolition. Imagine all the perks which people who work for the company have access to that could lead the company to financial ruin. One nice example is offered by *How to Fire Your Boss,* a web site devoted to workplace subversion: "BART train operators are allowed to ask for '10-501s' (bathroom breaks) anywhere along the mainline, and Central Control cannot deny them. In reality, this rarely happens. But what would management do if suddenly every train operator began taking extended 10-501s on each trip they made across the Bay?"

Get the cogs started churning in your head and you'll soon find many legitimate policies that can be exploited excessively to the company's detriment. The bosses might even decide to do away with the policy, which will upset the workers or customers who used to make use of that policy, and upset workers and customers are part of your goal anyway.

Attack #19. Waste Their Time

Time is money. The more of their time you waste, the more money they are wasting. One idea is to be on the lookout for job opportunities in the company. You and your partners-in-crime should apply for all the jobs you can. Compose dazzling résumés that perfectly fit the job at hand, with fake references and a winning cover letter. They will waste their time interviewing you for the job. Maybe they'll even offer it to you! Another idea is to send out dozens or hundreds of fake résumés to every job offer. They'll go crazy trying to weed out the legitimate submissions from the cranks. Here are some more wicked ways to waste their time:

- Write a threatening letter from an attorney saying a person in a publicity photo is suing, or accusing them of anything from plagiarism to copyright or patent infringement.

- Set up meetings or meals with key executives. Don't show. Or do show if the meeting is scheduled for their building — it'll give you an inside look at the place.

- If your company promotes itself as environmentally responsible (the way The Body Shop does, for instance), pester them with many embarrassing questions. Can they back up their claims? Exactly how much money is donated to the Abused Cockroach Taskforce? How many square miles of rainforest are we saving when we buy a box of Jungle Crunchies? Go to them directly, and go to their P.R. firm, and get the stats. (Whatever the result, you can use their answers against them. No matter how enlightened they are, they're not doing as much as they could be doing, or at least that's the way you'll make it out when you report this to the media!) Come to think of it, you can pester *any* company with embarrassing questions.

As they pursue these red herrings it will deter corporate executives from more pressing (real) problems of their business, and contribute to a worried corporate culture.

As I mentioned before, businesses are fragile things. Even the most steadfast and seemingly solid businesses have gone down. Smaller businesses are even more in peril. According to Dun & Bradstreet, "Businesses with fewer than 20 employees have only a 37 percent chance of surviving 4 years and only a 9 percent chance of surviving 10 years."[50] Consider this typical example: One of the busiest streets near my house has a strip mall where more than half the storefronts are empty. Stores have come and gone in that strip mall, again and again. They just can't seem to stay put. Even with a big name food store, toy store, and a bank in the strip mall to pull in crowds of people, the stores keep going out of business — and that's without any help from you!

Furthermore, some businesses are even worse, moans D&B — such as restaurants, which rarely survive more than two years (20% make it that far). Consider this one: A few miles away is a busy college town swarming with students, families, and rich doctors from the nearby hospitals. They all go to the main street to hang out at the bars and restaurants, and shop. Even with all these people coming and going, there are certain businesses that just can't seem to stay in business for very long. One store started as a pizza place, until it closed down and became a taco place, until that closed down and became a great Mediterranean place, which (you guessed it) closed down, and became a pizza place, which (guess what!) closed down, and was empty for a few months until finally it became an ice cream store. Right now the ice cream store has been in business about a month and I'm curious to see how it does.*

Across the street is the most telling example of all. There was a wonderful coffee house there, but it too went out of business. This was *the* coffee house. The coolest place to hang out, and everyone was there. There was a constant procession of people ranging in age from high schoolers to college students to the old men who sat for hours playing chess. The place was constantly packed with patrons buying overpriced coffee and cakes. Rock bands and special theme nights drew even more business. I really liked this coffee house. But one day I noticed the expensive prices were growing even more expensive than usual. The price of a plain cuppa coffee had doubled twice in the past two months. Incredulously I asked

---

* Late-breaking news flash: The ice cream store closed, and there's a sign in the window saying a hot potato store is moving in!

the owner what gives, but all he could do was shrug his shoulders and put on a hangdog look. He had to raise prices. And people still came. The place was always standing room only with lines spilling out onto the sidewalk one way, and out to the backyard in the other direction.

Then there were other changes the owner made specifically to increase profits. The interior was rearranged to allow more seating capacity. The cashiers took turns walking around like cocktail waitresses, asking customers if they wanted refills, seconds, or another slice of gourmet cake. The cashiers also tried to upsell customers. One day I came in to buy a root beer. She told me it would be great as a root beer float. (I'll admit, she seemed so honestly overjoyed at the prospect of a root beer float that I actually let her upsell me.) With all of these tactics — higher prices, increased capacity, upselling, and refills — the clientele remained as enthusiastic about spending their cash there as ever. It was quite a surprise one day, then, to come along and see the coffee house had shut down. The coolest, busiest, most active joint on the street, the one raking in tons of dough, had gone out of business.

"This is crazy!" I said to myself. How can a business that's raking in so much money, go out of business? The answer was simple. It didn't matter how much money it was taking in, it was spending a lot more than that. Even successful companies can be forced out of business because their very success leaves them in a vulnerable state: They need to spend more and more money on new hires, facilities, equipment, and maintaining their reputation, yet the influx of cash might not be sufficient to cover the outflux. Joan Rivers describes this as exactly the problem she had with her Tony award-nominated, successful Broadway show *Sally Marr*. The show "was theatrical magic," she wrote, "the reviews sounded as though I'd written them myself... There was, however, one problem: Though the show's raves were going through the roof, so were its expenses, and we were barely breaking even... And one black day I learned that there was no way to keep the show open. I felt a nightmarish unreality at seeing it closed with two days' notice. I was heartbroken" she concludes sadly.[51]

Or the money might be dribbling in, in such little drops that it's insufficient to make up for all the sweat and heartache that goes into keeping the business afloat. A similar anecdote is told about a Vermont entrepreneur who started a successful resort, only to go out of business. The more success he achieved, the deeper in debt he sunk.[52] As usual, money — or lack thereof — conquers all. Remember that as you plan your attack against the company you loathe so much: just get them to spend, spend, spend. That's all they have to do, is spend more than they take in, and their company is bound to close its doors eventually.

Citations

These are the books and magazine articles cited throughout the text. References with an asterisk (*) next to it indicates a particularly helpful or interesting work; or a work I just happened to like (though it may deal only tangentially with the topic at hand). Information with no citations was taken from a variety of sources including confidential memos and e-mails, policy manuals, system manuals, posters from company bulletin boards, and miscellaneous ephemera found in the desks and files of various corporations.

1. * Morgan, Hal and Kerry Tucker. *Rumor!* Penguin Books. New York. 1984. pp. 144-145. Light reference book that attempts to explain the truth and falsity of many popular rumors.
2. Schudson, Michael. *Advertising, the Uneasy Persuasion: Its Dubious Impact on American Society.* Basic Books. New York. 1984. p 94. Mostly dry study of advertising.
3. Schudson, p. 94.
4. Morgan, *Rumor!* p. 56.
5. * Morgan, Hal and Kerry Tucker. *More Rumor!* Penguin Books. New York. 1987. p. 183. The sequel to *Rumor!* containing more truths and falsehoods from all areas of life.
6. *Ibid.,* pp. 133-134.
7. *Ibid.,* pp. 137-139.
8. * Rosenbluth, Hal F. and Diane McFerrin. *The Customer Comes Second: And Other Secrets of Exceptional Service.* William Morrow and Company, Inc. 1992. pp. 185-186. Nice insider look at how Rosenbluth Travel treats its employees well, and reaps benefits from it. Written by the company's CEO and an executive at the company. It made me want to work there! Interesting analysis of the costs of employee turn-over on page 38.
9. *Ibid.,* p. 193.
10. Jones, Kasey. "Free Nikes, Missing Kidneys and Other Online Myths" in *The Star-Ledger.* Saturday, April 25, 1998. p. 39. Originally from *The Baltimore Sun,* this arti-

cle discusses some of the hoaxes and rumors that flourish on the Internet, such as the Gerber and Nike tales.

11. Morgan, *Rumor!* pp. 144-145.
12. Hendon, Donald. *Classic Failures in Product Marketing: Market Principles Violations and How To Avoid Them.* NTC Business Books. Lincolnwood, Illinois. 1989. pp. 89-90. Contains many stories of dumb things that companies have done to dig untimely graves for themselves.
13. Tough, Paul. "The New Auteurs" in *Harper's Magazine.* June 1993. pp. 33-45. Contains a forum where movie execs contemplate how they would sell an imaginary terrible movie. Great insight into the minds of Hollywood and how they convince the teeming masses that the shit they serve is foie gras.
14. Tough, Paul. "Hard Times" in *Playboy.* October 1986. p. 51. Jerry Falwell getting his number tied up by gay activists.
15. Winkler, John. *Pricing For Results.* Facts on File. New York. 1984. p. 120. Ho-hum book on pricing.
16. Hendon, p. 80.
17. Lewellen, Judie. "Movie Munchies: Snacking Sins in the Cinema" in *Sassy.* June 1995. p. 34. The popcorn boycott that plummeted sales.
18. * Kawasaki, George. *How to Drive Your Competition Crazy: Creating Disruption for Fun and Profit.* Hyperion. New York. 1995. pp. 117-118. Some good ideas, but not as subversive as the title might lead a sick mind to believe. Some of the best anecdotes are in a section called "Play with Their Minds," in which he describes devious tricks for deceiving a competing business.

19. Stauber, John and Sheldon Rampton. *Toxic Sludge is Good for You! Lies, Damn Lies and the Public Relations Industry.* Common Courage Press. Monroe, Maine. 1995. pp. 62-63. Scary tales showing how the public relations monster persuades people, politicians, and corporations, to believe things they would not ordinarily believe, or to take actions they would not ordinarily take.

20. * Sokolov, Raymond. *How to Cook: An Easy and Imaginative Guide for the Beginner.* Wings Books. New York. 1986. p. 61. Great cookbook for non-cookers; has the anecdote about Mr. Knopf's grudge against the French restaurant that eventually went out of business.

21. Yates, Scott. "Private Cleaning Companies Agitated by Inspections at Bragg" in *Fayetteville* (N.C.) *Observer-Times.* August 31, 1996. Cleaning companies at Army base complain that they're being run out of business by overbearing rules of inspection.

22. Dvorak, John C. "Inside Track" in *PC Magazine.* March 12, 1996. p. 87. Dvorak's column telling the twists and turns in the Taligent tale.

23. * Foreman, David. *Confessions of an Eco-Warrior.* Harmony Books. New York. 1991. p. 132. Manual of instruction for those who wish to protect the environment with monkeywrenching and tree-spiking type tactics.

24. *Ibid.,* p. 118.

25. *Ibid.,* p. 134.

26. *Ibid.,* p. 173.

27. Associated Press. "Thousands of Mink Die After Release by 'Ecoterrorists' " in *The Star-Ledger.* Monday, June 2,

1997. p. 2. Article about monkeywrenchers who released
minks into the wild to free them from becoming coats.

28. Foreman, p. 114.

29. *Ibid.*, p. 122.

30. Lewis, Kate Bohner. "Pity the Poor Mailman. Dr.
Reynaldo Fong to Serve a Year in Jail for Ordering
100,000 Magazine Subscriptions in Someone Else's
Name" in *Forbes.* June 5, 1995. p 21.

31. * Whitlock, Chuck. *Chuck Whitlock's Scam School.* Macmillan. New York. 1997. p. 9. Whitlock, who appears
regularly on many news programs and talk shows exposing scams, frauds, and cons, offers up every trick under the
sun.

32. Cherry, Matt. "Tabloid Hell" in *Free Inquiry.* Spring 1998.
News snippet mentions the dumb people who came to visit
the farmer's pit to hell.

33. Emshwiller, John R. "Desire for Revenge Fuels an Entre-
preneur's Ambition: How a Successful Partnership Went
Sour and Turned Into an All-Out War" in *The Wall Street
Journal.* April 19, 1991. p. B2. All information on Philip
Leslie and his war on the very company named after him-
self, taken from this article.

34. Furger, Roberta. "Don't Get Mad, Get Online: Consumers'
Ability to Air Grievances on the Net Has Forced Companies to Respond to Client Complaints" in *PC World.* October 1997. pp. 37-40. Article about poorly treated consumers fighting back with nasty web pages attacking the corporations that disgruntled them.

35. Office of the Federal Register National Archives and Records Administration. *The United States Government Man-*

ual 1997/1998. U.S. Government Printing Office. Washington, DC. 1997. This guidebook lists addresses and contact information for all the federal agencies you might wish to contact in your quest for business annihilation.

36. Taylor III, Alex. "Pep Boys — Manny, Moe & Jack: How to Murder the Competition" in *Fortune*. February 22, 1993. pp. 87, 90. Story on how Pep Boys tries to beat their competition into the ground.

37. * Barreca, Regina. *Sweet Revenge: The Wicked Delights of Getting Even*. Harmony Books, Crown Publishers, New York. 1995. p. 116. Contains lots of great revenge anecdotes.

38. Green, Larry. "At 96, Feuding Matriarch Opens New Business" in *The Los Angeles Times*. December 18, 1989. p. A1, A20-A21. Article about Mrs. Rose Blumkin who vowed to force her grandsons' store out of business.

39. Burrows, Peter. "A Nest of Software Spies? The Avant! trade-theft suit could begin to rein in Silicon Valley's freewheeling ways" in *Business Week*. May 19, 1997. pp. 100-102. Article about the Avant! company which allegedly was started up by stealing technology from another company.

40. *Ibid.,* p. 101.

41. Cohen, Andy. "Should *you* Steal *your* Rival's Reps? Luring salespeople away from the competition may have its benefits, but the drawbacks can be numerous" in *Sales & Marketing Management*. December 1995. pp. 60-63.

42. Brewer, Geoffrey. "I'm gonna be their worst nightmare" in *Sales & Marketing Management*. August 1996. pp. 42-48.

Tale of an ex-Xeroxer who fled to a smaller rival and vowed to beat the copy giant into the ground.

43. Gill, Michael and Paterson, Sheila. *Fired Up!: From Corporate Kiss-Off to Entrepreneurial Kick-Off.* Viking, Penguin Group. New York. 1996. p. 122. Primarily a book about entrepreneurs (this business of shutting down businesses is entrepreneurship of a sort, I guess).
44. Smith, Douglas. *Ever Wonder Why?* Ballantine Books. New York. 1992. p. 67. Questions and answers about everyday things.
45. Hofman, Mike. "Disco Nights End on a Downbeat" in *Inc.* April 1998. p. 29. Brief article details the failure of the Transylvania Restaurant due to its 17-month delay in opening, and supposedly the conservative community who opposed its disco nights.
46. Vogel, Carol. "Reopening in Midtown" in *The New York Times*. August 14, 1998. p. E32.
47. Dellecave Jr., Tom. "Insecurity: Is Technology Putting Your Company's Primary Asset — Its Information — At Risk?" in *Sales & Marketing Management.* April 1996. p. 40. Article about InfoWar Inc whose business is to steal corporate data; information espionage; and the risks of technology.
48. Sternitzky, Julius L. *Forgery and Fictitious Checks.* Charles C Thomas, Publisher. Springfield, Illinois. 1955. p 57. A retired inspector of the Oakland, California, Police Department reveals all he's learned in his 30 years investigating crimes of check fraud and forgery.

49. Hoffman, John. *The Art & Science of Dumpster Diving.* Loompanics Unlimited. Port Townsend, Washington. 1993. p. 27.

50. Cyber Media. "Some of the Reasons Why Businesses Fail and How to Avoid Them" in *Entrepreneur Weekly.* Issue 36. March 10, 1996. Internet publication at **www.eweekly. com** in which the Dun & Bradstreet figures on business failure were cited.

51. * Rivers, Joan. *Bouncing Back: I've Survived Everything — and I Mean Everything — and You Can Too!* Harper-Collins. New York. 1997. pp. 20-21. Rivers describes how even her successful show became unsuccessful financially. She also describes an incident where a company she bought went out of business because of the debt of its parent company.

52. Gill, p. 123.

benefits a legitimate employee would. Call up a few local temp agencies and tell them you would like to work for this company. Ask if they ever provide temps there as a way to get your foot in the door. Some companies hire "permanent temps," that is, temps who are hired by the company to fill in different jobs every day, wherever a job is available each day.

Breaking In #4: Plant Yourself In

Big companies have a plant service who come in every day to take care of the greenery. That may be another way to gain entry into the building.

Breaking In #5: Snack Supplier

Some smaller companies can't afford vending machines, but they allow a snack supplier to come in each week and deliver a cardboard box full of goodies. The box is filled with chips and candy bars, and there's a coin-box built in. Employees are on the honor system. They take snacks from the box and dump money into the cardboard receptacle. It costs nothing to the company, the snack vender gets to keep any profits he makes, and the company gets to eat any snacks they choose to buy. If you know your target business is small and hungry, you might see about getting one of these snack boxes and see if they'll let you drop it off in their kitchen or one of their back rooms. Then you will have an excuse to enter the premises each week. And once you're in... who knows?

Breaking In #6: Be a Friend

If you have a friend or relative in the place, then you'll have a means of entry, a contact on the inside, and an excuse for hanging around. If not, start cultivating friends on the inside (you'll need them anyway to gang-bang the company into oblivion).

Breaking In #7: Sell a Product

Big companies have vendors who come in to sell products. They set up tables of merchandise, usually near the cafeteria, and sell all through the lunch hours. Call the company and see what you can do to gain entry in this way.

Breaking In #8: Lecture

Some companies host lecturers who come in to speak to their employees. They host learning sessions, skill upgrades, and tutorials. Depending on your credentials and what you know, you may be able to sell yourself as a professional who can deliver a suitable lecture on some topic. Once you're in, sneak off and have the run of the place.

Breaking In #9: Back Doors

It never hurts to look around for a back door left ajar or unlocked, a service entrance, or a way of entering from an adjoining building. Sometimes a building is all locked up, but you can get in *next door* and sneak through an overpass or basement entrance into the place. There's often some kind of loophole like that just waiting to be discovered.

Breaking In #10: Piggybacking

An AT&T security guidebook told this tale: "In an AT&T facility, there was a rash of computer and software thefts. After an investigation, it was discovered that unauthorized people would piggy-back on employees' access cards [two people entering together on one ID] to gain entrance into the building."[1] People are usually nice enough to hold doors open for you. Pretend to walk in with them, as if they are your business associate. You'll want to ride up in an elevator furthest away from the receptionist or guard at the end of the hall, so there's less chance they'll see you. Preferably a crowded elevator.

Breaking In #11: Pose as a Customer

Depending on the company, you might be able to pose as a customer or potential client. At a high-tech firm you might say you're having problems with the software and need someone to show you the ropes. Let them lead you to the engineers, who are probably nice people and don't care much about rules anyway. Once you're done asking your questions, say, "I'll show myself out, thanks!" Of course, you don't really let yourself out! You use the opportunity to wreck the place.

Breaking In #12: Interview

Send a letter and résumé requesting a job, internship, externship, or just an informational interview. You might also pose as a journalist writing a book or article. At the very least you will gain a little access to the company, and will find out what it's like on the inside. At the very most you could end up with a job or internship that will allow you to infiltrate from the inside! Also, with interviews you can use your presence to mislead them by feeding them bogus information about trends, likes/dislikes, or about their competitors (if you pretend to work for their competitor you can feed bogus info about them).

Some of these techniques are best done with a partner, or even a group of people. Five of you might go in to sell merchandise, but only four actually stand at your booth. The fifth goes off and engages in industrial espionage.

"Visitors: Return Badges to Lobby Desk"

— so says the sign near the exit of many office buildings instructing visitors to return their temporary badges so they can't re-enter. Of course the guards don't care and never hold you to the sign. If you walk out with your badge, you can walk in again the next day using it. Guards are supposed to check the date and time written on the badge, but how often do they really do that? What this means is most of the time you need only procure one badge, even a visitor badge, and you can come back in again and again.

Some companies are smart about this. Ad agency Young and Rubicam passes out temporary sticker passes that become EXPIRED after a few days on exposure to air or light. If your target business uses these, see if you can store your stickers in a bag to prevent "spoilage."

Floor Plans

It might be helpful to procure floor plans of the place before breaking in. A realtor might have them, especially if they're leasing office space. I've even seen stacks of flyers in public lobbies with floor plans, maps, and complete descriptions of the building, either because the company was trying to sell their building, or they just wanted to brag about how big it is. This sort of information might also be available from fire departments or civil defense organizations who must be informed about building designs and hazardous materials stored there.[2] A friend of mine who volunteers at the township fire department told me about plans for a fundamentalist religious organization building being built nearby long before any of the newspapers got hold of the story, because he had access to those plans and others, months in advance. Find your company's plans, and you can plan on getting in to pay them a destructive little visit when they least expect it.

Citations

1. AT&T Security. *The Security Seven: Your Guide to Protecting AT&T's Treasures*, p. 2. Little security guide given to AT&T employees. The story about the manager who overheard competitors discussing him was from here but originally described in *Arizona Business Gazette*, June 29, 1995.
2. *Washington Researchers Publishing. *How Competitors Learn Your Company's Secrets.* Washington Researchers, Ltd., 2612 P. Street NW, Washington, DC, 20007. 1990. p. 29. The provocative title says it all. Ostensibly this is a manual for protecting one's own business, but it can be used as an idea sourcebook for industrial espionage techniques. I borrowed heavily from this great manual for the chapter on industrial espionage.

Inside Jobs

Now that you know some methods of gaining access to the company, our attacks will start to make use of your special inside privilege. The following attacks are designed to drive them out of business by wasting the company's money, and the employees' time and patience — from the inside.

Attack #20. Maintain a Revenge List

Lester Timmons was a timid man, a loyal employee, and a schlub. One day he realized his life was going nowhere, he would never be offered a raise or promotion at work, and his wife treated him like the dust under a doormat. He decided to take action. He started to maintain a revenge list. That's the idea that propels *The Man with Fifty Complaints* by Mary McMullen.[1] Lester carefully records every damaging piece of gossip he can find on everyone at his company. He's very careful, taking his lists home with him each night so as not to be found by meddling co-workers. He records the boss who steals office supplies; the comely assistant whose promotion seems proportional to time between bedsheets; and forty-eight other complaints about his peers and the corporation they work for.

You can maintain a revenge list of your own, recording all the filthy little secrets you come across while investigating the place. The company insiders in your corner can help pad out the list (more on that later). Once your list begins to grow, taunt the head honchos with it. Blackmail the people involved. Then make it public. Use a company directory to find all employees and send them copies of your revenge list, and send some envelopes to shareholders as well.

One more thing: In the novel, when Lester's co-workers started feeling intimidated by the list, he got threatened, framed as a cheating spouse, kidnapped, conked over the head, and nearly strangled to death. Of course, that was just a novel.

Attack #21. Random Acts of Violence

You can go around overturning desks and chairs, chopping down doors with hatchets, and smashing walls to pieces. However, those sorts of activities, while fun, are obvious attacks against the company. Your attacks should be sneakier. Not so obvious. They should be the kind of attacks which cause employees to become angry at their work environment, while creating lots of unproductive downtime and wasting money. But they should never, ever, suspect it's because of sabotage. Here are some examples:

- **Unscrew them.** Unscrew backup emergency lights, or replace them with burnt out bulbs. They'll be left in the dark if a true emergency hits.

- **Itching powder.** Sprinkle liberally on the toilet seats and in cloth chairs and cubicle walls. A little thing like that can lead to serious sickness, out-of-work cases, and lawsuits.

- **Plants.** Poison all plants on premises, thus driving up the costs of their plant service. Start a rumor that something foul is floating through the air vents. This is an attack that will breed suspicion and mistrust among the employees and management.

- **Rotten food.** Plant raw fish or ripe bananas in inaccessible ventilation shafts. In the middle of summer.

- **Show them a good time.** Piles of boring women's magazines in the waiting room? Glue in the most offensive pornographic pictures randomly throughout.

- **Flood them.** Dump out bottles of correction fluid on keyboards, phones, and other equipment.

- **Destabilize them.** Steal one wheel off the bottom of every rolling chair.

- **Bug them.** Let loose a swarm of ants or other insects in their place. Some agricultural catalogs sell cans of bugs to farmers to help their plants grow. Or go to your favorite woodsy area and start turning over rocks, or leave out some sugar to attract insects. Come back a little later and collect the bugs. Won't that company be distressed to find they've got insects crawling all over the place!

Imagine how great it will be if you plant dozens of little time bombs like these all around the company, once or twice a week. Pretty soon the workforce will become dispirited, upset, angry, and frustrated. As their unease grows, they will become more and more resentful and productivity will decrease. They will become snappish. They will be more inclined to leave the company, steal office supplies, and do stupid things to get themselves fired. All actions that are beneficial to your cause.

Attack #22. Cut Off Their Communication

Personal attacks inside the company should also focus on destroying interpersonal communication with each other and customers. These are little things, which means you can do them quickly, but they make a big impression. Every person in the company — all of your foes — will be slowed down immensely.

- Print up fake copies of employee directories filled with mistakes (or just steal everyone's directory). They'll have a harder time communicating with one another.

- Sever their phone cords.

- Erase or misprogram auto-dial phone numbers stored in the telephone system.

- Remove the cardboard inserts from telephones that show whose line is ringing.

- Steal Rolodexes, or steal some of the important cards out of them.

Imagine if you do all this during their most competitive times of year. Think what a terrible time they'll have over the next days, weeks, or months, as they try to get themselves organized again. And while they're struggling, you'll be continuing to attack in other ways. This ability to make your pranks have a large and lasting effect is what turns pranks into meaningful steps towards destroying the business.

Attack #23. Pour Their Cash Down the Drain

If you want to waste their money and drive up their costs, try some of these techniques:

- Leave their water running. Just leaving the water dripping and sprinkling overnight, every night, will add up to wasted cash over time. You might also be able to "fix" the sinks so they can't be completely shut off.

- A leak-auditing company called Utility Survey Corp estimates that a tiny .2-inch hole in a pipe can cost a company $1,945 per year as water leaks away into the ground. A crack little more than an inch can cost the company $2,891 per year. Utility Survey Corp reports dollar amounts that grow progressively higher as the size of the crack increases... so get digging!

- Remove any water-saving devices they've installed, such as bricks in the toilet tanks or special faucet attachments.

- Turn their heat up — way up! Try it over a three-day weekend and they'll return to a particularly hellish environment.

- Some office kitchens are equipped with an oven. Leave it on a little, as if someone had forgotten to shut it off. You can turn on a gas range so gas escapes but no flame is there to burn it, creating a noxious and dangerous situation.

- Before you leave for the night, be sure to set the microwave to the highest cooking time. It will churn away for a few hours or so, wasting precious energy, but by morning it will have shut off with no evidence it was ever turned on at all.

- Leave the refrigerator or freezer door open a crack (or more than a crack). A good way to do this is to rearrange the food so the door doesn't close properly. People will think they're closing it, but really it's staying open all the time.

- And of course, make sure you leave all the lights on.

You probably don't want to do all this at once, for it would be too suspicious. But if you have continuous access to this place of business, make sure to use some of these tricks whenever you can. They are the kinds of invisible destroyers that are impossible to detect as sabotage, and yet slowly eat away into profits.

Attack #24. Destroy Their Backup Tapes and Disks

Any half-intelligent company keeps careful backups of their computer files. The backups might be on disks or tapes. Some companies rely on individual workers to backup their data. A computer company I worked for backed up their entire computer system weekly onto tapes. An accounting office in my area does a nightly backup, also on tape. If their computer system should ever fail, all the data is stored on the backup tape.

If you infiltrate the company and find backup tapes or disks, there are a few options available to you:

- Get a bulk eraser or strong magnet to erase the tapes or disks.

- If they have a shredder, rip out the magnetic tape and feed it into the shredder.

- Another idea is to introduce errors into their spreadsheets, misspellings into word processing files, or viruses into their backup data.

- If it's a software company the backup will probably contain listings of the programs they're working on. How fun it will be to introduce bugs and glitches into their software! Minor changes can make a big difference. Change 1 to -1. Change colons to semi-colons. Remove a parenthesis or a quote mark here and there. Programming errors can be extremely costly to track down and repair. According to security expert Ira Winkler,[2] a one-line blooper in the Bank of New York's computer system resulted in a crash that led to a $5 billion shortage of cash, which had to be borrowed, whose interest ($23 million) then had to be paid. Not many companies could withstand a monetary attack of that magnitude.

- Of course you can simply steal the backup disks or tapes. The data might be useful and interesting — especially if you release it to their competitors.

Learn From Their Mistakes!

A 34-year-old man in Hartford, Connecticut, tried this tactic after being laid off from his job at an Internet company.[3] His bosses were pissed that he was starting up a rival firm so they kicked him out the door. That night the man sneaked in and erased all the company's computer files and backups. The company was almost erased out of existence, and in fact it lost some of its clients, but was back in operation within four days. The man was arrested and charged with felony computer crime. Here's what the man did wrong:

- **He bragged.** Although the man denies it, his boss says the man bragged he was going to destroy all their files.

- **He didn't hide his stuff.** The police found a customer list in his home (apparently it was a customer list stolen from his former employer). We know better — we have to hide things like that, even when they're in our own homes.

- **He didn't wait.** His biggest mistake was attacking the company the very night he lost his job! If he had waited a few months, the link to the disgruntled employee would have been less obvious and he would be less likely to get caught.

There is an interesting twist to the story. The arrested man claims he is completely innocent. Let's consider this possibility. What if the man really was innocent, and it was his former boss who staged the incident to draw sympathy for his own company and discredit the fired employee? Indeed, the fired employee said that his former boss was irked at him for planning a rival firm. So perhaps this wasn't a case of the fired employee trying to put the boss out of business — maybe it's the other way around — maybe it was the boss's way of putting the other guy out of business, even before his new business could take off!

- An even better idea is to create phony look-alike disks or tapes, with pornography or other embarrassing or illegal stuff on them. Now hide these fake backups in someone's desk — someone pretty high up in the company, but not so high that they're beyond reproach. How about a sales manager, low-ranking vice president, or other executive?

Now that you've got their backup data in the greasy palm of your hand, it's time to do the real dirty work: mess up their computers! When they find their computers or files are gone, they'll go to the backup data — but lo and behold, that backup data will be vanished, destroyed, buggy, error-filled, or whatever your nasty mind came up with.

Attack #25. Janitor's Closet

Look for the maintenance or janitor's closets. Some enterprising con artists have used the disguise of a janitor to make off with all sorts of office equipment. Chuck Whitlock writes about the "trash and dash" he pulled on a company in Oregon. Dressed up in a janitor's uniform he wandered in with a suitable uniform and a phony ID badge. "When the offices emptied at the end of the day," he writes, "I proceeded to pick up laptop computers, diskettes, ledgers, calculators, telephones, and other office equipment. I even found the corporate checkbook in the controller's office, and customer records in the sales office. *How easy it would be for someone to blackmail this company if they had this information,*"[4] he thought. And he did have the information, and apparently it was not too hard to get either.

There might be a sink here you can let overflow, or supplies to steal. But the best use for a janitor's closet is in conjunction with some "disgusting attack." If you do a disgusting thing (i.e., leave a stomachfull of vomit on the President's desk before his big meeting), a nice bonus touch is to first "clean out" the janitor's closet, hiding the mops and buckets so they can't clean up the mess. A nice way to pick up some gross stuff is to steal medical waste from the metal boxes in front of doctors' offices. Needless to say this can be extremely dangerous to one's health, so be careful. But once you've got it, feel free to strew it around the desks and offices of the people you love — least.

Attack #26. Mail Cubbyholes

Some offices have cardboard or wooden cubbyholes where mail is inserted for each worker. These offer a handy way to grab mail as you pass by. Take it home with you to read at your leisure. Anything that's not too useful (like junk mail), just throw it in a public mailbox and eventually it will be re-delivered to them. Anything that *is* useful you can keep, read, and exploit against them. Another use for cubbyholes is to see who habitually doesn't pick up their mail. That's important to know because you don't have to return their mail as quickly. (Someone might not be in the office too frequently, or they might be on vacation and have a huge accumulation of mail.) That's a clue you should target that person's office or cubicle for an investigation, since they're unlikely to surprise you as you're snooping about.

You'll hit the mother lode of customer letters in the company's complaint department or customer service center. Remember the old saying about business — each dissatisfied customer goes on to tell six other people about the bad experience he had with the company. That's why you'll want to intercept as many letters as you can from customers and reply to them yourself. Of course you'll write back to them using all the tact and diplomacy of a pro wrestler (see sample below). You have a few choices:

- Don't respond at all to the customer (causing them to fume and seethe and get even more heated up).

- Respond inappropriately. Don't reply to their questions. Everyone loathes not being listened to.

- Respond in an out-and-out hostile manner. Don't overdo it or they'll suspect it's a prank.

> Dear Customer:
>
> Sorry to hear you're dissatisfied with our service and wish to cancel. Too bad we can't do that. You signed a contract and we're sticking to it. If you don't like us, you can use our competitor's service (call them at 888-555-1234). Finally, we are adding a $550 charge to your bill for "false cancellation claims." Thank you and have a nice day.
>
> Regards,
> [Signed by bigwig executive of your company.]

If you run a competing company, make sure the company you wish to see fail doesn't have any of your promotional literature lying around. If so, check your customer database. Make sure you're not sending stuff to their home addresses (they may be trying to fake you out by using their home address instead of the corporate address.) Mail also tells you if they're searching for a new office, new vendors, or are planning certain strategies. That's why you'll also want to...

Attack #27. Tail the Mail

Tail mailroom staff on their rounds, as they push their carts around the office. Find the weak links in that chain of events. For example, are there certain times on the journey when the mailroom clerk leaves the cart unattended while he chats up a young secretary? (Add it to your revenge list!) Or does he periodically stop into the bathroom, leaving the cart unguarded and free for your perusal? Such times are perfect for you to make off with ultra-important mail and memos to executives. For instance, maybe you spot the logo of a consulting firm on an envelope. You snatch it up, steam it open, and find it contains an invoice for fees rendered. With some of the forgery skills you learned earlier, you remake the letter, adding extra digits here and there, especially under the categories of "Miscellaneous Expenses," "Travel, Lodging, and Meals," and "Office Support Staff." Now put it back in the mail. The receiving end of this letter may grumble a little and pay it off (wasting money); or grumble a lot and complain (causing friction). Either way, you win.

Another idea. After you get an executive's credit card data (like from a file cabinet), call the company and cancel the card, saying it was lost or stolen. Now you'll have to vigilantly tail the mail. When the new card comes (or when the letter comes from the company confirming deletion of the old card), you grab that letter and card out of the mail cart, before the executive gets it. Bravo — you now have full access to the boss's credit card. (You may need some confidential information, like a Social Security number, to activate the card. But that's what all this espionage and snooping around is for. Hope that the executive doesn't try to use his old card before you get the new card.)

Finally, many companies have delivery boxes in the lobby or outside. Intercept those deliveries however you can. You might be able to break into the box (see my book *How to Hide Things in Public Places* for information on breaking into FedEx and UPS lockboxes[5]); or sometimes the packages are carelessly stacked on top and around the boxes, especially when they're too big to fit in the slot, or the drop box is full, or if you stop up the opening so no one can drop anything into it. Take outgoing packages and you'll prevent customers from receiving the product, and, boy, won't they be P.O.ed about it.

Attack #28. Becoming Buddies

If you have any sort of inside connections to company employees, you can use them to find out more about the business. There is all sorts of info that can be helpful to your cause. Is there a back door they keep unlocked (or will keep unlocked for you if you ask)? Are there any weaknesses that can be exploited (like computer passwords, or a potential client sale which is wholly dependent on one salesperson getting to the meeting on time)? By becoming friendly with the guard at one place of business, I slyly found out about certain lax security policies. From talking with a technician I found out about underground network cables buried outside the front of the building. A little spadework and the cables could be severed, impeding the company's computer operations.

- **Joking around for info.** Joking around can lead to valuable information. While temping at a technical company, I wanted to know how far I could go without being caught on security cameras. I didn't see any cameras, but that didn't mean they didn't exist. I befriended a higher-level technician and one day asked him if he had any strategies for one of the games on my computer. Of course I knew he would jump at the chance to show his skill. While he was goofing off, I said, "The best part is, they're watching you here hard at work, all on the security cameras." He chuckled and said, "Naw, naw. The only security they got around here is the one I put in by the front door." "Really!" I said. And I had exactly the information I needed.

- **Bitching against the boss.** Another way to get employees on your side is to bitch (kindly) against the boss, or against bosses in general. As you're talking to them (in person or on the phone), do so in a way that shows you understand that their bosses are tyrants who have weird quirks. Find out about them while proving yourself harmless.

- **Making nice.** Many salespeople use the trick of buttering up "gatekeepers" in order to gain better access to the high-powered executives. They act genuinely friendly towards the secretary, receptionist, or assistant who stands in the way between the executive and the outside world. After many months of persistent niceness, they are finally in a position to shame the secretary into letting them finally speak to the boss: "I'm shocked that Mr. Quimbles would treat me so rudely still after all this time!" they might say, or "Come on, Mary, can't you do me this one little favor? Surely Mr. Quimbles must have five minutes to spare some time or other." You can use this sort of technique to gain access to executives for some of the attacks throughout this book, for instance in order to show them you are an intelligent consultant who stands to earn them a ton of money if they'd hire you for your business advice (ha ha, little they know what evil you've got up your sleeve!)

Attack #29. Dangerous Things

Look for accidents waiting to happen that you can exploit, or accidents that can be set up. Dangerous things leave a company tiptoeing on a bridge made of fragile eggshells over a high and rocky valley.

- An important presentation left in front of an open window? Oops, I wonder how that got there.

- Investigate what happens to factory waste, chemicals, noxious stuff, that emerges from the premises. Can their waste outlets be plugged up or diverted back into the company? Would local residents or agencies be interested to know what's pumping out of that building?

- Fuse boxes can also be helpful, especially if they're used to turn off all the lights in an emergency.

- Some fire extinguishers are hidden behind a column or in a niche — hard to see — especially when you take down the sign. Slice fire hoses lengthwise while you're at it, or chop 'em in half, or whatever form of slicing and dicing helps best express your castration anxiety. Not only damaging, but could also open up the company to all sorts of liabilities as well as fines.

- And of course, always be on the lookout for any nasties that can be added to your revenge list.

Attack #30. Anti-Positioning

As you study the company and indulge in espionage against them, you're sure to find out or figure out the way they position themselves in the marketplace. To those cave dwellers out there, "positioning" was a big buzzword a few years ago in business circles, and I still think it's an idea that's right on target. Businesses try to position themselves with a certain image. It's how they try to fool you into buying their product. For instance, a soda is never just a sugary drink. It's always something that will bring you to a refreshing tropical island (7-Up); or distinguish you as a hip, urban, young person (Pepsi); or mark you as a non-conforming iconoclast (Sprite). All the big companies do this. They make you think of their product as somehow a little different than all the other products (even though all the products are pretty much the same thing). *Specifically because* all the products are pretty much the same thing. They feed you this imaginary difference between Coke and Pepsi, or Sprite and 7-Up, or Nike and Reebok, or whatever. Pick up on these false facts they attempt to create, and see how you can belittle and undermine the position they create for themselves with them.

With all the snooping around you're doing, you're going to be holding firm to the handle of their positioning tactics. Find their position and attack that. Create a fake business newsletter that shows how people are *against* the trend they are positioning. Ever-vigilant corporate suckasses will read the newsletter and show it to their bosses with signs of concern on their foreheads. Whatever you can do, do it. They will waste time/money/resources as they reformulate their positioning campaign. It's disinformation, baby!

Attack #31. Copy Rooms

The room full of copy machines can be put to all sorts of devilish purposes:

- Slight adjustments to copy machines will cripple them and the business. Editorial and art departments use copy machines a lot, as do book agencies. Poke holes in toner canisters for color copiers. It is severely crippling when they don't have access to their machines. Bend or break the mechanisms that guide the paper through the machine. Then they have to feed it all by hand, or wait around for a serviceman to visit.

- The recycling bin might have useful information in it (is someone making copies of their résumé?). If something's being copied it's probably important to some degree, so seeing what's being copied might help you target your espionage activities against the firm.

- At night, after everyone's gone home, set all the copy machines to the largest size paper, lift up the cover to expose the copier glass, and set it to 999 copies. Then scram! It will start pouring out yucky black sheets, wasting paper and expensive toner cartridges. Of course, you could just steal the damn cartridges but this messes with their minds too.

- And of course the copy room is valuable to you because it will allow you to photocopy ad campaigns, employee data, spreadsheets and strategies — any data that can be used against the company, or can be used by their competition. Be careful when copying that someone doesn't sneak up behind you and demand to know what you're doing there in the darkness of night!

- Let's say you've snuck in and are furiously photocopying pages from a top secret presentation binder. Here's a tip to help you save time in the dark of night. Turn to the back of the binder. There might be computer disks there in plastic holders, which contain the report. Just swipe the disks and you can move on to other things and get out of there more quickly.

Attack #32. Fax Attacks

Copy rooms usually contain at least one fax machine. Individual offices or cubicles might also have fax machines. Go around to each one and try these fax attacks:

- Collect the faxes that have just come through, and the other unanswered faxes sitting around gathering dust that no one has responded to yet. You can take these faxes and reply to them. "Dear Customer: (Don't give them the dignity of actually inserting the customer's name in the letter. You really should start it with: Dear Customer.) The problem you reported in your last fax isn't too bad. We've heard worse. We'll work on it if we have time and let you know if we solve it…" Sign your response with the name of someone important who you want to get fired.

- There is often a pile of recently sent faxes nearby, which is useful for snooping through so you can see what is being sent to clients and business partners. Some fax rooms have product literature or other oft-faxed documents out for the taking, which may assist your industrial espionage attempts.

- Also, while you're at each fax machine, take a look at the phone number used to reach that fax. The phone number might be written on the machine itself, or it might be on the wall jack, or there might be a list hanging on the wall. Now that you have those fax numbers you can place free ads in local newspapers and on the Internet informing the public that they should fax photos of their genitals to those numbers. The photos probably won't fax through very well, but that's okay, the main point is to wear out their fax machines, use up all their toner, and tie up their lines.

- Fax machines are programmed to print the name of the company and fax number at the top of the page. That's no good, you'll have to reprogram them! Alter that fax number and name of business to print out whatever nasty message your deviant mind can dream up. There should be an instruction manual nearby the faxes to assist you with this.

- While you're at it, reprogram all their auto-dial buttons. The secretary thinks she's faxing the top-secret memo to her boss's boss, when in reality she's sending it to the NBC *Nightly News.*

- You could slice the fax cable or cord, but that would make the above three ideas a waste of time (why reprogram their auto dial buttons if the cord is cut so they can't send faxes?). So only do outright damage like this if you can't do the other kinds of fax attacks.

Attack #33. Undo Their Ads

Marketers and admen have a saying: "Good advertising kills a bad product." That means if it's a bad product with good advertising, people will buy it once because of the good advertising, but they'll never buy it twice because they found the first time what a bad product it was. To put it another way, if their product tastes funny, is difficult to use, doesn't do the job, or is otherwise below par — customers will find out quickly enough by the good advertising and word will get around. So if you're in the Out-of-Business business, you can allow the company to have good advertising — as long as their product is bad or if you can *make it bad*. But a bad product + bad advertising is best of all.

Notice that the "good advertising kills bad product" idea only works when the customer is smart enough to effectively evaluate the product. If they're buying something as mysterious as life insurance, medicine, or mutual funds, for instance, customers may continue to buy bad products because they don't know enough to make sound judgments about quality.[6] Those are the cases where other tactics might better be employed.

As part of your industrial espionage campaign you will certainly find out what ad agency or public relations firm is used

by the company. Some of your best information might come
from attacking that ad agency, their garbage, rifling their files,
and so on. If you can get a glimpse of the ad before it goes
out:

- Look to see what the purpose of the ad is. Is it to announce
a new product? Announce a price change? A special deal?
Reaffirm the consumer's belief in an old product? Keep
the company's name in their mind? Different purposes reveal what the company is trying to achieve, and in turn different purposes command you to respond to them in different ways.

- Take measures to counteract the ad, prevent its effective-
ness, or change its impact. For example if the ad relies on
a joke you could try to do something to make the joke
seem ill-advised or offensive. You could also take the
stance that this is a critical problem that should not be
dealt with by a company that jokes around.

- Anyplace the company advertises, write and call protesting
the company or products (see also Team Tactics later on).
Express disgust to the magazine or radio station that ac-
cepts their advertising.

- Go around and pick up all the flyers and posters the company distributes around the city. Remove their inserts from
newspapers. Deface signs and billboards.

Only do these things when the company is riding high. If the
company is taking a beating by the media you might use that
to your advantage. Let them advertise so their ads will be associated with the controversy (meanwhile exploit the controversy for all it's worth). Companies often cancel their adver-

tising to keep their names from being permanently linked in the public's mind with the bad news. Airlines often withdraw ads after plane crashes. Hitachi and Mitsubishi canceled ads in Japan when a scandal broke out concerning industrial espionage. "There is no admission of guilt by pulling [out] advertising," said one Mitsubishi executive. "But when your name is linked to something like this, you are not going to flaunt it in front of everybody."[7] *Au contraire* — *you* will flaunt it for everybody!

Attack #34. Gaslighting

"All too often companies bring stress, fear, and frustration to their people — feelings they bring home with them each night. This creates problems at home which people bring back to work in the morning. The cycle is both terrible and typical,"[8] warns Hal Rosenbluth, CEO of Rosenbluth Travel, and author of *The Customer Always Comes Second*. This cycle of stress and problems is so bad, it led him to put the customer second and his people first, as he says. Later he says: "We are consistently able to trace higher costs to cases of unhappiness in specific departments and offices. We take it very seriously."[9] Of course it's *your* goal to create such stress. Gaslighting (causing employees to doubt their sanity) is one way to do it.

While rummaging around (see "An Employee's Desk" chapter later on) you will gather lots of data on people. One way to use it is to help identify who will be most mentally distressed by subversive mindgame tactics and then target those people. Is someone's desk super neat? Try moving something slightly on their desk. Tomorrow is it back in the original place? Boy, are they anal retentive. On their computer are they heavy users of encryption and passwords? Do they lock their desks and bring the key home with them? These are all people whom you should target for mental mindgames, as they are paranoid and high-strung. The higher up in the company you find 'em, the better.

Now that you've found some target people who are likely to explode, exploit those character traits and quirks. Deliberately take one thing off or from inside their desk each day, like a Very Important Piece of Paper that they worked overtime the night before finishing up. Another day you can leave a vague and threatening note on their desk — a cryptic "You'd better shape up" should do nicely. For some paranoid types it may be enough to simply knock over the books they have placed neatly between two bookends, or rearrange the items on their desk so they'll suspect they're being spied upon at night — and they'll be right!

Some people have a regular pattern that can be exploited. Like, they always go to the bathroom every day at the same time, leaving their pocketbook unguarded. Or the executive who works out in the company gym every day during lunch time, leaving his briefcase and pager in the locker room.

Choose specific people to gaslight, and specific actions that will affect the company. For example, if you link together someone's paper clips, it might drive them crazy but it won't put the company out of business. If that's what your goal is, choose people to gaslight whose distraction will harm the company. (If the president gets sidetracked from his goals to pursue silly stuff like that, it is damaging to him and ultimately wasteful to the company.)

A young woman I knew went crazy because her hard drive seemed to crash every day and she would continuously lose all her hard-done work. She was a particularly valuable employee, but she couldn't concentrate, couldn't work, and couldn't get things done because she had to spend her day alternatively trying to repair the damage and keep herself from exploding. These things build up. Minds unravel at the thought of redoing all that work again. She quit before long, and the company was set back by her loss. At another company, where important documents kept seeming to disappear from the hands of one executive or the other — and then reappear in the other one's office — the two ladies got into such heated battles with each other that everyone else was too frightened to work with them and they withered in their jobs for years, not contributing much to the company, and adding plenty of aggravation to it, until finally being fired from their posts by a new CEO. Driving employees crazy by various means will hurt the company as much as it hurts them, and is quite entertaining to watch too.

Attack #35. Warehouse or Product Shipping Center

If you can infiltrate the warehouse or product shipping center you'll have direct access to the product before the customer receives it. That means you'll have the chance to mess up the product somehow or other. Make it broken. Make it dangerous. Make it faulty. Do it enough and the customers will start getting the picture and word will get around that this company's selling garbage. You might even provoke a lawsuit against your least-favorite company, and if lawsuits come about, surely their liability insurance rates will increase, and as the final indignity, the company might decide to recall the product. This last is especially humorous since it is a self-imposed attack the company brings on itself.

Is there a spare roll of shrink wrap you can borrow to wrap the faulty products? Environmentally incorrect Styrofoam peanuts? Look around the place and you can use all their own ingredients to go into the packaging. If it's a software company, do they have disks laying around? Disk duplicator machine? Instruction manual for the duplicator? You can take it home and study it so that when you come back at night to dupe off the virus-infected disks you'll know precisely how to use it.

It looks really bad if they have to recall a product, so you want to keep the company in the dark as long as possible. I mean, if they find out right away that their product could cause serious injury to children, then all hope for massive lawsuits against the firm is lost! Eventually a recall and replacements will come about. Oh, they'll try to make the most of it, they'll try to impart a spirit of integrity, using the incident as a positive ad campaign ("We are such a wonderful company who stands behind our products and even recalls them when there's the chance they'll kill ya..."). But the consumer knows the truth: the company loused up, and now they must pay the price.

You want to fight every possibility of the company making the most of a recall, before they have a chance to spring up. If you send out enough faulty product, you can also go back to their original program, CAD/CAM design, blueprint, or backup tapes, and make changes which imply that the original product was flawed in some way. Thus the company might feel compelled to recall the product. This is good for you because a recall means substantial loss of profits and substantial costs in getting the word out to the public that the product is being recalled. If it's a large enough recall they may have to develop a "recall center" or a facility where the recalled products and refunds can be processed. They also have the problem of having to deal with all the faulty products (or products they believe might be faulty). Either they'll have to throw it away, which is wasteful, or they have to inspect each item carefully to see if it really is faulty, which is also wasteful. Either way they're in a bind, and you're the one tightening the knot.

Here are some more ideas for the warehouse, product shipping center, or mailroom from where packages are sent out:

- Leave behind lots of heavy packages to mail out. These can be full of bricks, dog crap, or broken products which are to be sent to very influential people.

- Damage their postage meters. Besides costing money to replace them, they will have problems sending out products. The company will have to waste time as an employee trots away from his work to the post office to mail packages.

- Look for incoming packages that can be re-routed. For instance if a customer is returning a product, you can "lose" it so that the customer gets doubly annoyed. Or you can replace the return with an even more costly item, so the company ends up crediting the customer with more than was originally paid.

- If they pack cartons with crumpled office paper or newspaper, stuff in some of your own incendiary tracts against the company.

- Look for product that is waiting around to be sent out to customers. Remove key pieces from the set, so as to render the product defective and infuriate the customer.

Attack #36. The Firing Line

Every time an employee leaves the company your tactical plan grows a new set of wings. It doesn't matter if the employee leaves amicably or is fired. It doesn't matter if they switch to a new job (but it's nice if they switch to a competitor), or if they retire. All that's important is you do everything in your power to force employees out of the company. Why? A few reasons:

- **Every employee is in opposition to your cause.** The less employees there, the less enemies opposing you.

- **Expenses of new hires.** When an employee leaves or is fired, it creates a lot of time-consuming work for the human resources department and for the person's supervisors. Ads have to be written and placed in the newspapers. Job hotlines have to be updated. Forms have to be filed. Candidates have to be interviewed. Background checks must be done. Rejection letters have to be sent out. It's a lot of time-consuming and costly work to be done, and it keeps everyone away from more productive matters.

- **Expenses of new employees.** Once a new employee is hired, it takes a while for him or her to get "up to speed." They make mistakes in the beginning. They're unproductive. They take away time from managers and co-workers who have to train them. Time and money must be spent to update their e-mail, voice mail, and to print stationery, business cards, nameplates, and ID badges. They are paid a salary from the beginning, but they're not worth the money they're paid for several months.

- **Loss of customers.** When salespeople jump ship to a new company they often take their old Rolodex with them and transfer their clients. One business consultant wrote about a dental practice that moved its office a few blocks, only to find his busy practice dropped sharply. He couldn't understand why a few blocks to a fine new location would make such a difference. **Answer:** *It didn't,* not to the patients, anyway, but it turned out a part-time receptionist had decided she didn't want to take the extra bus to the new location so she didn't transfer with the practice. The practice had lost a friendly and engaging woman who reminded patients about appointments, booked them for new appointments, and kept the customers coming. The downturn in business was so profound due to her loss that the dentist was willing to pay taxi fare to get her into work — and the patients started flocking back.[10] *Never underestimate the importance of anyone. Even a part-time worker can cause major consequences.*

- **Discontent.** Employees leaving for any reason create discontent. Layoffs and firings create unease in the remaining employees, as well as the employees who were axed. Even in the case of a retiree or simple job-switcher discontent is created, as one person is promoted to fill the empty slot and everyone else is passed over for promotion. (Even worse when no one is promoted to the slot and everyone else does double the work to pick up the slack.)

You can see how very costly it is every time an employee leaves a company, and how much time is wasted on trivialities (I've read estimates that it costs a company over $3,000, and sometimes as much as $10,000 to hire a new employee).[11] Think of what would happen if the top salesperson was fired from a company. It might take a month to hire a new salesperson. During that time, the company loses out on all the business the top salesperson would have brought in. The company also loses because many of those customers will stay loyal to the salesperson and shift with him to his new company, wherever that may be.

It doesn't even have to be the top salesperson. I spoke with a representative at a multi-million dollar company who told the story of what happened when the *bottom* salesman was fired for not making the grade. When he left it required a restructuring of his sales territories. Superfluous meetings were held, binders prepared, evaluations done, and all manner of scrutiny was given to the most trivial details. It even led to meetings with the company president and CEO — the biggest big kahunas in this whole empire. In other words, that one firing led to a ton of work and wasted time and effort for everyone from that salesman's peers all the way up to the top brass. The fired salesman's territory got divided up among the already overworked remaining salespeople. They resented the extra workload, and ignored their new territories since they didn't know the customers, had no rapport with them, and didn't "buy into" the changes. Some of the salespeople didn't even know the value of their new accounts. One salesman ignored a $100,000 account because he thought it was worth much less than that. You can see how one measly firing can have major ramifications.

A few months later I spoke with a different salesperson at the same company who was laid off along with hundreds of her co-workers. The division's building was shut down, and only three or four members were being retained by corporate headquarters. The division was effectively out of business due to mismanagement. When she told her customers about the layoffs, many of them became so irate they refused to do business with that company ever again.

For all these reasons it is imperative that you do everything in your power to find out who the best people are at the company, and then *get them out of there.* Find the top salespeople, the creative thinkers, the smartest problem solvers, and use these techniques on them:

- **Gaslighting and random acts of violence.** Use the techniques of gaslighting and random acts of violence discussed earlier to create an unsavory atmosphere in the firm for specific people. They will be more receptive to wanting to leave.

- **Headhunters.** If you really have located the best people in the firm, a headhunter will like to know about them. That was the method used by a high-ranking executive at a major firm who was ready to kill his boss and was ready to quit. Instead of quitting or killing, the executive went to a headhunter the next day and told him to find *his boss* a new job. The headhunter went along with the plan, found a new job for the boss, and he was hired away by the other firm.[12] You could try the same method on an effective higher-up in the firm, then sit back and let the job offers start rolling in. He may not actually accept any of the jobs, but you can at least let it slip to *his boss* that he's thinking of leaving. That might brand him as a disloyal traitor, and he will find himself on a slippery slope on the way out of the company.

- **Check their references.** Find the name and number of the company's best employees *then find the name and number of their bosses*. Call up the boss and say you're doing a reference check on the employee. Especially if it's a small company the boss will get pissed that his hotshot is trying to get another job.

- **Fake it.** Why don't you call up the salespeople (or whomever) and ask them if they're interested in changing jobs. Set them up for a fake interview. You can even meet with them, talk with them, offer them a grand salary, offer them the job, and ask them to start tomorrow. They will quit their jobs, and — Surprise! — have no new job to turn to. How cruel! But that's the world of business for you. (By the way, conducting interviews is also a form of industrial espionage; it's a great way to find out insider information about a company.)

- **Appeal to their creativity.** People in certain fields, such as advertising or publishing, or in certain departments, like art departments, are probably creative types who feel like they could be doing a lot more than their current position allows. Play on that sense of unfulfilled creativity, and offer them the lure of better outlets for their creative juices at other companies, where the rules are less stringent, and the individual spirit is highly valued. That's all bullshit of course, since no one values anyone's individual creativity, but no matter what company or position they're in, chances are the grass will look greener on the other side.

Citations

1. McMullen, Mary. *The Man With Fifty Complaints*. Doubleday & Company, Inc. Garden City, New York. 1978. Mystery novel about a man who compiles a list of fifty items intending to use it to destroy his company and co-workers... and angers one of them enough that they want to destroy him.
2. Winkler, Ira. *Corporate Espionage: What it is, Why it is Happening in Your Company, What You Must do About It*. Prima Publishing. Rocklin, California. 1997. p. 40. Grand slam stories on the front lines of corporate espionage, including many of Winkler's own adventures.
3. Lynch, David J. "Ex-employee Charged With Cyber-Crime" in *USA Today*. December 19, 1996. page 1B. short article on Internet company ravaged by enraged former employee.
4. Whitlock, Chuck. *Chuck Whitlock's Scam School*, p. 138.
5. Fiery, Dennis. *How to Hide Things in Public Places*. Loompanics Unlimited. Port Townsend, Washington. 1996. Contains an extensive discussion of breaking into UPS and FedEx drop boxes.
6. Schudson, Michael. *Advertising, the Uneasy Persuasion: Its Dubious Impact on American Society*. p. 19.

7. *Ibid.*, pp. 116-117.
8. Rosenbluth, Hal F. and Diane McFerrin. *The Customer Always Comes Second: And Other Secrets of Exceptional Service.* p. 10.
9. *Ibid.,* p. 36.
10. Wright, Harold L. *How to Make a 1,000 Mistakes in Business and Still Succeed: The Small Business Owner's Guide to Crucial Decisions.* The Wright Track. Oak Park, Illinois. 1990. pp.115-116. Self-promoting book by a business consultant. Contains the interesting anecdotes about the doctor and dental practices whose businesses declined or rose based on a change of location.
11. Winkler, Ira. p. 305.
12. Michaud, Ellen. *Boost Your Brainpower: A Social Program to Sharpen Your Thinking and Ageproof Your Mind.* Rodale Press, Inc. Emmaus, Pennsylvania. 1991. pp. 99-100. Methods of sharpening your mind.

Special Tactic Report: Industrial Espionage

One of your first attacks — an attack that continues through and throughout your vengeance — should be industrial espionage. Industrial espionage means finding out useful information about a company. Almost any information can be useful if you can figure out a way to use it. Washington Researchers publishes a report called *How Competitors Learn Your Company's Secrets* (don't worry, I'll tell you all the good parts). They say that based on the research projects they've undertaken for clients, most businesses want to know their rivals' overall strategy, financial situation, costs and sales, new developments, what new markets are targeted, and information on sales staff and R&D personnel.[1] Certainly these are all greatly valuable pieces of information to find out if you're running a rival business or if you're merely trying to run a company out of business. After all, if you can get to their target markets before they do, or if you can find a weak link in their strategies, all the work they're doing in those directions will be for naught.

Public Sources

Espionage usually begins with publicly available sources, which sounds like a drag but can really contain a wealth of information. You see, most people don't bother going after this stuff so they don't realize all that's out there. Even companies don't know what secrets can be discovered about them from public sources. You might remember a few years back when Bell South spun itself into a tizzy when hackers distributed thousands of dollars' worth ($79,449 to be exact) of "top secret documents" through an e-mail mailing list.[2] The hackers calmly pointed out that the same information could be purchased from the company for $13 by calling their 800 number!

- Find out if the company publishes any information at all that they will send to you — flyers, sales literature, catalogs. You may have to use a friend or family member's name and address to protect your anonymity.

- Once you've gotten a company directory you can look up names in computer databases to see if anyone's publishing. Executives might publish articles in business journals. Engineers and technical types might publish in scientific or computer journals. Anyone might publish in a local newspaper.

- Press releases and news items can usually be gotten from the company's public relations office. If you approach them right you might be able to weasel away with explanations and excuses about all the different scandals the company has been involved with the past ten years. You may even find out negative stories about the company you didn't even realize existed before speaking with them.

- Basic library research, by searching computerized data-bases for mentions of the company, are always fruitful. You could find interviews with company personnel, newsworthy revelations, or hot gossip. There are also databases that give general information about businesses, such as the number of employees, revenue, and other data.

- Books, magazines, newspapers, professional journals, industry bulletins and newsletters. While researching this book I've come across hundreds of little gems in all these public sources, that are easily overlooked, but would make queasy the corporate stomach if those nuggets were found out or more widely known. I found out about the big name retail store that uses no security tags on its merchandise. I found out about the ways a low-level employee bilked her boss for thousands by using her company's own bureaucracy against them.

Businesses make disclosures of all kinds to federal, state, and local government offices. Sometimes for legal reasons, other times they may release information to persuade the government to act on their requests positively and quickly.[3] Some examples of public data include:

- Public offerings.

- Government bids.

- Patent and trademark registration.

- Building permits, proposed plant expansions, and details about what will go on in those plants. Sometimes companies must apply to the Federal Environmental Protection Agency (**www.epa.gov**) or state or local agencies which then make even more private company data available to the public.

- Collective bargaining agreements for companies are available from the U.S. Department of Labor, detailing data on wages, job categories, and vacation policies. Also available is a wealth of information on the company's pension plans, which year vested employees leave the company, plan financial statements and funding data.[4]

- Products sold to the government, how much was sold, and at what price; this data available from the Federal Procurement Data Center.[5]

- Tax assessments from the local tax assessor's office can reveal the estimated market value of a company's buildings and equipment, the size and uses of each building.[6]

All these things become part of the public record, and may contain hints about a company's plans for the future, the inner workings of their technologies, and their goals.

Certain industries must file for applications with the Federal Communications Commission, or Food and Drug Administration (**www.fda.gov**), or other government agencies which then make the applications publicly available to your prying eyes. Other companies might ask governments for special services or money, and in the process release information of all sorts that can be used against them.[7] If the company is ever investigated by the U.S. Occupational Safety and Health Administration (OSHA), the Federal Trade Commission, or the Antitrust Division of the U.S. Justice Department, those reports may be placed in the public domain, freely available to anyone who cares to look for them.[8] Companies who partner with universities might find data leaks in the typically generous nature of an academic environment, as well as the fact that much research done with certain schools is available through the Freedom of Information Act.[9] If they do have any data you're entitled to by FOIA (or for that matter, any reasonable questions you have about the company even if not covered by FOIA), request it. If they come forward, then you'll have the data. If they don't come forward their reluctance looks quite suspicious — ammunition to use against them when you take your case to the media, picket line, or web. And finally if company executives ever testify before Congress, the U.S. International Trade Commission, or for certain government studies, those remarks too become available to the public. "Many Office of Technology Assessment reports reveal substantial details about specific companies in the industry — information shared by those companies' executives."[10] There are plenty of detective books out there that go into great detail on how to look up this sort of information.

📖 *Get the Facts on Anyone: How You Can Use Public Sources To Check The Background Of Any Person Or Organization,* by Dennis King. Prentice Hall. New York. 1992. One of the many detective type books available, this one tells about all the sources of information available to the general public — if you know where to look for them.

▣ **www.sec.gov** U.S. Securities and Exchange Commission's web site allows you to search using EDGAR (their Electronic Data Gathering, Analysis, and Retrieval system) to find all the forms companies are required to file with the SEC. Easily pulls up pages and pages of info, often requiring plenty of patience to sift through.

▣ **www.dialog.com** One of the best, and best-known, sources of on-line information (but it costs money to use). Allows searching of over 500 databases, containing data on businesses, market research reports, news, and much more.

On Premises

Your espionage can continue on company premises. Check out their bulletin boards. Look for signs of picnics, meetings, "getting to know the customers" functions, product seminars, betting pools, and embarrassing things (racist jokes, anti-customer postings, and other stuff that would be embarrassing if made public).

- The smoking areas outside office buildings often teem with insider gossip, complaints of the day, and shared anecdotes.[11] And usually smoking areas are fairly accessible to anyone who cares to stand there and inhale the fumes.

- Go on corporate tours of the company. Study carefully any weaknesses in their security arrangements. Perhaps you can even walk off the tour.

- There might be a visitor's log in the reception area that can be stolen or at least glanced at.

- It's easy to infiltrate a company picnic or softball game, and sometimes holiday parties. See whom everyone is fawning over, study their faces carefully, and listen to what they have to say.

- Often there's an abandoned cubicle or unused office or room with junk in it. This can be used as a "hideout" inside the place, a cache spot. There may be a computer there or you might be able to look through old paper files in that abandoned office.

Funerals

Keep an eye on the company flagpole — half mast? Maybe a jet went down with executives in it. Check obits and news articles. Funerals are places where many employees, managers, executives, and family gather. Attend funerals to listen in, spread rumors, and for general information gathering. Also it may be useful just to know the names of dead people who can't speak out against lies you tell about them. If nothing else, when an employee's out of the picture that leaves a gaping hole in the firm, a department that becomes one person short, and perhaps a little easier to target with other sorts of attacks. Remember the first three letters in funeral spell F - U - N!

The Classroom

Your research should uncover if any company executives teach lessons. They might teach college classes, adult education, weekend seminars, or perform at trade shows. Of course they'll use internal company anecdotes in their lectures, so it may be worth signing up for their classes to get an inside look at the firm. An alternative is if you know someone in the company especially suited to teaching, you might persuade them to do just that. Many adult education schools, like the New School in New York, and local schools elsewhere, are constantly looking for new teachers who can lead exciting courses. If you can send them the necessary forms to apply for the job, along with an encouraging letter and some ideas, they may just take on the task and you'll gain from it. There are other public forums where executives might speak — club meetings and community groups for example, so keep an eye out for such events.

Telephone Troubles

Most competitive secrets are learned directly from company employees or from people associated with the company who mean well but don't know any better, such as suppliers, customers, or joint-venture partners of the target company.[12] It's a fact that people who deal with the public, like sales reps and customer service agents, sometimes don't know how or when to "shut it off." It's their job to divulge information, and for that reason they can be vulnerable to outside forces wishing to delve into company secrets. Some companies have corporate libraries filled with data — and corporate librarians who love fulfilling a caller's information request.

At AT&T, Corporate Security investigated a case where an unknown person masquerading as an AT&T vice president called and asked to speak with the president of the business unit. He got the secretary instead, but that was okay, because from her he found out the specific department he was interested in, and she was nice enough to transfer him there. The person who received the transfer was now looking at an internal call apparently from a company official, and had even more reason to believe the slick charlatan on the phone, and the employee "cooperated in providing sensitive information."[13] Personally I've called companies many times, asking all sorts of questions. Of course I tell them I'm writing a book. You can too. Just tell them you're writing a book and want to ask some questions. Other investigators have used other ruses to ask nosy questions. Pretend you're a business major doing a project. A magazine intern fact checking data for a story. Maybe you're affiliated with a TV or radio news program and wish to have some preliminary information preparatory to asking an executive on your show. Or a corporate headhunter searching for just the right candidate for an unbelievable job offer. Alan Greenberg, chairman of the board of The Bear Stearns Companies, sent around one of his famous memos warning staff:

> There is no question in my mind that people with no affiliation with Bear Stearns have been calling employees of Bear Stearns and... These impersonators have requested confidential information... They... call the low-level associates... and identify themselves as an important Bear Stearns Sr. Managing Director and try to get information that no one but a few Bear Stearns people should possess... We are in our own war with people who do not mind destroying our customer confidentiality to achieve their own personal goals.[14]

If you ask the right people, ask the right questions, you'll get some good answers. Just don't let their boss find out.

Questionnaires

So you want information, kid? How about just come right out and ask for it? That's what one Japanese company did. They sent questionnaires to some U.S. competitors, saying they were thinking about using the firms as their supplier, but they needed more data first to make up their minds. Now, as you know, wave the banner of foreign money around any American businessjerk and he'll respond accordingly. The questionnaire asked for detailed explanations of corporate locations, names of people who worked each place, and sensitive information on the products developed there.[15] The Americans faithfully, greedily, provided all the requested information. A French firm twisted the tale a little, inviting companies to bid on a contract job — but wouldn't ya know it? — in order to bid, one had to prove to the Frenchies that their company could meet the demand, and that required providing all sorts of sensitive information about their firms. After getting all the info they wanted, the French company "changed its mind," deciding not to award the job to any of them.[16]

"What Can I Do with All This Data?"

Now that you've got all this data, what can you do with it? For starters, lots of the attacks throughout this book can be enhanced by using data you find during these investigations into the company. For instance, your rumor-mongering will have an air of authenticity if you base them on facts you disclose. There may be company secrets you can dish out to the media. You may do as one consumer activist does — use databases like the SEC to find shareholders and use that as leverage against the firm (wouldn't it be bad if you started writing letters to all the major stock owners, speaking evil of the firm and pleading with them to sell their shares?).[17] You might discover news of a corporate merger — and wouldn't the other company like to hear some of the secrets you uncover? Or perhaps the company is being investigated by some pesky government agency for something or other — how about some anonymous tips to brighten their day?[18]

If you find marketing plans, see who they will be targeting and you can try to undermine it. They're trying to sell to elderly: put up warning signs in old age homes, tell 40-year-olds not to let their parents patronize that business, and report them to AARP.

Any business deal will have a swarm of confidential memos and paperwork circling around it. How horrible it would be for the company if some of the details were leaked during the midst of negotiations! In one corporate communiqué I found the tale of a company forced to move, who had decided they were going to move to one particular building, and that was the only building they had in mind. The owner of the new building strung them along, then decided the building was not for sale. After pressuring the owner, he finally agreed to rent the building — for $7 million higher than the original agreement. In another case, a building owner misrepresented a building as being ready to be moved into, when in fact it needed two months of major renovations. The business was forced to pay rent for the two months ($180,000) when they couldn't even occupy the building. In both these cases, said the executive who wrote the memo, the deal was soured for the business because the owners of real estate are "normally very shrewd. If they know we are in a hurry and that we have no other options, they take advantage of us. Also, fitting-up

space is often a hidden but significant cost (and time consumer), which should be fully understood before real estate
investment decisions are made." You can see how even the
most innocent of information (that an owner is anxious to
move, or that they don't have a back-up plan, or that they've
overlooked needed renovations) can be quite useful to the
other side of the bargaining table. Furthermore, it's important
to note that the fact that a buyer who has overlooked the need
for renovations is not something you're going to see on any
memo. It's something that you, as an intelligent sifter of data,
have to pick up on, recognize as important information that
will screw the company if you tell the other party about it. So
you're not just looking for the data that's there, you sometimes
have to read between the lines to discover what they haven't
thought through, what they haven't noticed. And then you'll
find the loopholes in their plans — and the means to destroy
them.

Suppose you uncover a sales presentation. You can see their
key sell points and try to beat them, or to alert rival companies
how to beat them. Companies have found that by analyzing
their marketing plans before putting them into action, they can
usually come up with several ways their competition might
undermine their plans and blow them out of the water. "We
were really blown away by their ability to match our technology and market plan," said one executive after one of these
brainstorming — and plan busting — sessions. "We realized
we did not have five years to work with this plan, but actually
just two."[19] Obviously if they hadn't taken the time to think of
all the sneaky ways their plans could be smashed to smither-
eens, they would have dragged out the five-year plan and gotten trampled less than halfway home. The same tactic was

used to defeat President Clinton's health care reform plans. Opponents to the plan used opinion polls to uncover what aspects of the plans were unpopular, thus coming up with a list of vulnerabilities. They then formed over twenty different coalitions, each one specifically formed to attack one particular vulnerability in the plan.[20] The point is simple: Most companies don't do all this extra thinking and planning, and so they're a little more vulnerable anyway. Add to that the fact that with all this espionage under your belt you'll have insider knowledge of their plans and schemes, and so will be in a great position to grab the sledgehammer and smash away.

Citations

1. Washington Researchers Publishing. *How Competitors Learn Your Company's Secrets.* Washington Researchers, Ltd., 2612 P Street NW, Washington, DC, 20007. 1990. pp. 7-8.
2. Barlow, John Perry. Crime and Puzzlement. Available at various Internet sites, such as www.eff.org. An article that will make you angry about injustices against computer hackers.
3. Washington Researchers Publishing, p. 16.
4. *Ibid.,* p. 17.
5. *Ibid.,* p. 16.
6. *Ibid.,* p. 16.
7. *Ibid.,* p. 19.
8. *Ibid.,* p. 21.
9. *Ibid.,* p. 26.
10. *Ibid.,* p. 22.

11. Winkler, Ira. *Corporate Espionage: What it is, Why it is Happening in Your Company, What You Must Do About It.* Prima Publishing, Rocklin, California. 1997. p. 10.
12. Washington Researchers Publishing, p. 9.
13. AT&T Security. *The Security Seven: Your Guide to Protecting AT&T's Treasures.* p. 7.
14. Greenberg, Alan C. *Memos From the Chairman.* Workman Publishing. New York. 1996. p. 90. A collection of memos from the Chairman of the Board of The Bear Stearns Companies, Inc.
15. Winkler, Ira. p. 67.
16. *Ibid.*, p. 99.
17. Bruni, Frank and Elinor Burkett. *Consumer Terrorism: How to Get Satisfaction When You're Being Ripped Off.* HarperCollins. New York. 1997. p. 90. How to make companies take your consumer complaints seriously — and what to do if they don't.
18. *Ibid.*, p. 91.
19. Carey, Robert. "Stiff Competition" in *Performance Strategies,* a special supplement inside *Sales & Marketing Management.* March 1996. p. 4. Short article espouses brainstorming about how the competition might undermine your company's marketing plans.
20. Stauber, John and Sheldon Rampton. *Toxic Sludge is Good For You! Lies, Damn Lies and the Public Relations Industry.* Common Courage Press. Monroe, Maine. 1995. pp. 96-97.

An Employee's Desk

Now that you're inside the company you have access to many of the employees' cubicles, offices, desks, and computers. You can gain a lot of crucial information from them. Even if it's just a lowly secretary or administrative assistant, you are bound to find much of value in your quest to overthrow the company. For example, a "lowly" administrative assistant puts together a spreadsheet that is used in an official report — but company decisions are based on that very data.

Use your insider status to do data collecting. Who is low-down but does crucial work? (Secretaries, mailroom.) Who is low-down and does morally-uplifting work, work that keeps spirits high? (Grounds keeper, janitors.) Who is high-up and does important work? (Sales leaders.) This knowledge is beneficial in determining who to target for attack. Companies like to say everyone is important — that's true — but we can exploit that. We look for the importance in each job and see how it can be used for destructive attacks. What kinds of attacks, you ask...

Attack #37. Names

Look in Rolodexes and in date books, and pop-up address boxes. Look for friends, family, work contacts, vendors, doctors, and any others. All can be helpful to you, your anti-organization, and the company's competitors. For example, a boycott or rumor attack might send literature to the people who work at the company, and their friends and vendors. I've looked through Rolodexes and found cards for "Psychic" and other potentially embarrassing stuff. Wouldn't it be terrible if some crucial employee was found to be making expensive time-consuming calls to her psychic while she was supposed to be working? Another use is to look for people's nicknames which you can use when telephoning to help make yourself look "in." And as you're looking around, don't forget to start pulling out a Rolodex card here and there, or ripping a page out of the databook. Crumple them up in your pocket, and walk away. You'll leave that executive as confused as a fish out of water.

Attack #38. Desk Plans

As anyone who's ever worked in an office knows, secretaries are the brains of the place. Especially the old ones, who've been with the company thirty-five years plus. They know everybody's secrets, all the tricks, all the loopholes, and how to get things done. The best are effective and efficient, and they know it. And they like to share their knowledge with others so they write up a Desk Plan, or a Guide to This Desk.

Or maybe it's called a Job Description. One way or another, they are so efficient that they've got time on their hands to spare, so they sit down and type up descriptions of how to perform their job. Some large companies require a desk description to be drawn up by each employee, but others do it as a congratulatory way to pat their own back.

You can find lots of helpful information in a desk plan. I've got one here I pulled from the desk of a secretary (let's call her Sheila) at a Big New York City Ad Agency. It is geared towards a temporary worker or someone filling in for Sheila when she's away. The first page starts off by listing Sheila's name, phone, fax, computer login, password, Audix extension and password (Audix is a kind of voice mail service), and some account numbers. See, already this has been worthwhile!

Page 2. Sheila starts describing the principals (executives) whom she supports, listing their names, titles (vice presidents, account director, etc.), employee number, and other useful account numbers. "Henry is the highest ranked executive at this desk," she writes, "therefore the work delegated by him takes precedence over everyone else's. He travels often... always keep a copy of his itinerary in the folder marked 'travel arrangements' then after the trip put them in the binder marked 'travel.' You will do this for each principal." So we've picked up some more useful tidbits here. Later on we will discuss Travel attacks in the chapter called, you guessed it, "Travel."

Over the next several pages, Sheila continues writing about each executive, telling their likes and dislikes, how they behave, what their spouses are like, and what work she does for them. All this is useful to varying degrees; it might help with a scam, with gaslighting, or just making you look like an insider. There are also other pointers to further information, like this about another executive: "If needed, John's home address and phone number, as well as various account numbers are in the Rolodex under 'C'."

Of another executive she writes: "He is very particular about his phone calls, because of his high rank in the company he will often get calls from the president of the company, etc. Take messages... and give them to his secretary... Unless asked otherwise, do not leave them in his Audix." Once again we see how useful information can be found herein. I'm sure you're now dreaming up all sorts of inventive ways to misroute calls, make sure he *doesn't* get those important messages from the president, and other methods of manhandling internal communication amongst these executives.

The next page contains some damaging information on her co-workers. I'll bet Sheila never thought anyone but another secretary would read:

> **Scott Hamilton** He is the VP of Advertising for [large fast food chain]. He is the client that will usually call Henry. Do not be offended if Scott is short with you on the phone. Scott does not take time to be polite when he is feeling stressed....

> **Matthew Mettlar** This one is a doosey. He is the Marketing Director for [large fast food chain]. He is a cantankerous human being, he is very rude. He will often yell on the phone, as well as curse, etc. Fortunately, he will not call often. But when he does, the same rules apply to him as to Scott. Be as polite as possible with him. If, however, he acts or says anything rude... tell Henry immediately.

You can add items like these to your Revenge List for future usage. Knowing who the volatile customers are will surely help because those are ones who will be easiest to turn against the company (see attacks #67 and 68 for examples).

After the people profiles, Sheila goes on to describe more useful facts that only a secretary would know. She talks about where and when a certain daily sales report comes in, and who it is to be distributed to (too bad that you'll intercept it, fudge the numbers, and drive everyone crazy!). She talks about where all the important documents are stored on the computer network. And she provides summary lists of important information about the company, and the people who work there.

The rest of Sheila's desk plan describes how to rent cars (at company expense), how to book airline tickets, and how to send mail and FedEx materials. Once again this is all the kind of stuff you need to know so you can have the company pay for all your expenses as you drive it over the edge of a cliff.

Not all desk plans will be as inclusive as Sheila's is (thank you Sheila!), and some might even contain more information. But I hope I have convinced you that if you do no other industrial espionage, merely swiping an informative desk plan can be all the data you need to get your mission accomplished, for it contains all the damaging information you could need in one convenient location.

Attack #39. Secret Numbers

Computer passwords, FedEx account numbers, credit card numbers, and other secret stuff is routinely stored in Rolodexes and scheduling programs. Schedulers may also have a teleconferencing number and code number listed in them, so you can get in on a phone meeting and listen in. Change their voice mail message and listen to the old and new messages stored there. Change their password.

- Some companies give managers special "order numbers" they can use to order products free from the warehouse. Usually this is for salespeople needing samples, or executives trying to make deals. You can use the number to order products for yourself, for friends, for strangers, for the competition. Or have them shipped to non-existent addresses.

- Get others involved who don't even know they're getting involved. After finding their credit card numbers, distribute them anonymously on the Internet. Within a short period of time there will be people all over the world using these numbers. Dole them out slowly so the problem lasts for a long period of time.

- Post computer dial-in lines, BBS numbers, and voice mail numbers as challenges to hackers.

- Some companies make it their business to sell information, such as through CD-ROMs or dial-in databases. If you can find the IDs and passwords used by company insiders, you'll be able to find and distribute that information free to anyone who wants it. There are some web pages devoted to revealing the codes used to unlock computer software without paying the full price for it, and you can add your contribution to those lists.

- If you find out the Social Security Numbers of any individuals (especially higher-ups) of the firm, these can be misused to make those people's lives miserable.

In one desk I found a handy manual called "How to Use the Z1100e Security Control," which was a guidebook to the company's alarm system, and which I photocopied immediately. The front has some hand-scribbles on it where some security-conscious soul wrote down a series of code numbers that represent different areas of the building. Page 3 gives instructions on arming the system, which is not too useful except for the fact that someone wrote the secret code number in the manual. Page 5 tells how to turn off the alarm, as well as "What To Do If The Alarm Sounds." The rest of the manual gives further instruction on programming and using the device, including how to change the code number. Wouldn't it be funny if every morning for the next several days, as workers trod into work in the morning, the silent alarm goes off in the monitoring station, bringing the police out to the place. The cops reprimand them for bringing them out to this false alarm, and the person who deactivated the system (with the old code number) feels embarrassed at having flubbed the code number. Of course, they don't know what the new code number is, so they're stuck with no way to turn off the alarm each day.

Attack #40. Vanish Plain White Envelopes

Hal Rosenbluth wrote about how just by making a few small changes in their use of supplies, his company saved big money. An associate in his firm "calculated we could save up to $100,000 per year just by using plain white envelopes for internal purposes as opposed to our letterhead envelopes and by always using the smallest envelope possible. So far, his idea has saved the company more than \$22,000."[1] You want to run this operation in reverse on your target firm. Figure out the cost-cutting programs in operation then sabotage them. Get rid of their "plain white envelopes," and their smaller envelopes, and the company will be forced to use their more expensive, larger, logoed envelopes and paper.

Steal supplies. Or damage them beyond repair. It's probably best to "lose" them if at all possible, so there's no chance they will send them back for a refund. You should also order tons of supplies on other peoples' account numbers (which you got from the desk plan or Rolodex). Make sure to order the most expensive, *heaviest,* supplies in the book. Have them shipped to competitors if possible.

- Slit open all their padded envelopes (the ones stuffed with shredded powder of gray pulp). This makes an incredible mess and is extremely annoying. Heck, slit open *all* their envelopes.

- "Accidentally" pour bottles of ink onto their beautiful corporate letterhead.

- Publicity departments are sometimes stocked with pre-stamped envelopes, or envelopes that have been run through a postage meter. Make off with these, use them to send out false recall notices ("We've recently discovered that some of our products are highly combustible, cancer-causing, and contain toxic kryptonite..."). If you have access to the postage meter itself you can really have a ball delivering malicious memos at their expense.

All these little things can add up to big costs, especially when you help them use up their supplies a lot faster than they would on their own. One chairman of the board whose dander is perpetually up over this issue is Alan Greenberg of the Bear Stearns company. In his book *Memos From the Chairman,* a collection of his memos sent out over the years, this is a theme that comes up again and again. Greenberg is big on watching "little" expenses like rubber bands, paper clips, inter-office envelopes, toilet paper, and his memos stress this point repeatedly. Even though he's the top banana in a pretty big bowl of fruit he still recognizes how harmful wasteful practices are. His memos constantly mention competing companies that have gone out of business — one reason being, he theorizes, because they didn't watch, cut, and reduce these sorts of expenses.[2] Business owners must, every day, pledge allegiance to the bottom line. With attacks such as these, and perseverance, that bottom line will rise higher, and higher, and higher...

Attack #41. Keys in Desk

Most employees are extremely stupid about keys. They keep spare keys in the top drawer of their desk where anyone could take them. See where the keys lead you — into locked file cabinets, closets, storage sheds, desks, computer cabinets, company vehicles, vans, cars, and lawn mowers, the bathroom, archives, or wherever. If it's kept locked, it's bound to be valuable in some way!

- If you get keys to the front door, or to outside storage sheds, make several copies of the keys and distribute them to punks who will absolutely destroy their place from the inside out.

- Before you leave, make sure you lock every door, every desk, every disk box, file cabinet, and anything else that can be locked. Then lose the keys, switch them around, or substitute keys that don't fit the locks.

Attack #42. The Haves, and the Have-Nots

The personal stuff that adorns an office or cubicle can be instrumental in your espionage activities. For example, while sneaking around in one company I noticed lots of environmental stuff on the wall of one executive, as well as a postcard from a Jewish organization. Each of these are clues as to her interests and means to attack her. For example, they might indicate she belongs to certain ecological or religious clubs, which would be perfect places to start building rumors of mistrust against her.

Look for hidden stuff in offices. In the bottom of a file drawer of one office I found a long lost pair of black panty hose. Planted in another's office or briefcase such a thing could cause havoc. Once I found an office with an automatic door remote control (and his secretary had one too). I knew *he* was important. A signature stamp can be used for forgeries, or for showing you what the handwriting looks like to make your own forgery. And in tightly controlled offices where a computerized key card is required to operate the photocopier, steal all you can get to shut down their workflow over the following days. Now that you've looked at what they have —

Look for What They Lack

They don't have a stapler in their office? Don't have a computer? Have a computer but no printer? Look at these as possible gripes. They may also provide the means to create disturbances. For instance, have the computer-less one fill out a requisition for a new computer or send her literature describing the benefits of a new computer. If they don't have something, what does it imply about them? Do they wish they had it? (Jealousy.) Are they unproductive because of that lack? Does it force them to go into someone else's office a lot to use that computer or that stapler? (Can be the basis of a rumor that the two of them are conspiring something together.)

Attack #43. Photo Intelligence

Look for photos of kids in front of a Christmas tree and the like. These are handy for informational purposes, and may also provide ideas for ways to drive employees crazy, or add to their discomfort. Suppose, for instance, a key employee on a busy day has to run to the school because she's received a nerve wracking phone call saying her kid got beat the hell up and is sitting in the nurse's office with a broken arm... nasty, huh? Look for photos of people on walls, company newsletters, or even oil paintings. Another use is in the airport limo-scam, and meeting scams discussed later on, so you'll know what the people look like to help you impersonate them at meetings and also so you can tail them.

Company newsletters may have photographs, as well as other personal information. For instance you can find out when certain employees are retiring from the company. Senior executives may "soon be on the consulting circuit,"[3] which means they may be delivering lectures in which they give away useful information about the company they've just left. Others who are leaving may afterward not feel the need to be as tight-lipped as when they worked for the firm, and so can be easy targets for confidential information using some of the interview scams discussed earlier.

Attack #44. In and Out Baskets

Let's take a look at what people are sending out in their Out Baskets, as it may include stuff that can be sabotaged, or may contain important clues such as a purchase order for ad space in a magazine. What would happen if you secretly double the order? Triple it? Now let's look in the In Bin. Is there anything there you would like to intercept before the employee gets a chance to look at it? Anything you should maybe *steal* so he never gets to see it at all? How about destroying the memo from his boss, or the note about the mandatory meeting Friday? These are the sorts of tricks which destroy communication, and can get somebody fired, both of which are exactly what you're aiming for.

Attack #45. File Cabinets and Files

Notice what cabinets/computers/doors/drawers stay opened-/turned on/logged in/unlocked at night and on weekends, and what's in them as well. You can put together a whole informational document on the company's unlocked loopholes.

You'll know more than they do about their weaknesses. Share your report with other members of your team so they too can benefit from the information out for the taking. As you look around their file cabinets you're sure to find all sorts of useful stuff like company directories, papers, reports, and —

Credit Card Information

Credit card statements and receipts of employees and customers. If it's customer receipts, you'll want to use the information to place bogus orders (or cancel orders). If it's employee receipts, especially a company credit card, circulate the number and expiration date widely so as many people as possible make purchases on it. In offices of executives who travel around you might find hotel bills, which often list phone calls made from the room. Follow up on this and you'll find out who exactly that executive was calling while away.

Business Plans

These might give financial overview, gross and net profit statements, company objectives and the actions to be taken to accomplish them, upcoming promotions, and a schedule for the upcoming year. However, warns Faye Brill, president of the Society of Competitive Intelligence Professionals in Alexandria, Virginia, even if you manage to put your wily little paws onto a copy of a competitor's strategic plans, it may be worthless as the plan might not be working, or the company might be straying from their plans as problems come up. "What's more, decisions based on incorrect information can be expensive mistakes."[4]

Holiday Memos

Every year a memo goes out stating when company holidays are. Know this and you'll know when the building will be empty and perhaps when employees will be out of their homes. Also tells when the building closes early, like the day before Christmas or New Year's. Also it helps to know when there will be less people in the office to spot you trespassing (like if there's a three-day weekend, maybe go the day before because lots of people make it into a four-day weekend). Also on some holidays companies go lax on admissions policies as the company is overrun by spouses and children. As one corporate memo stated: "Due to the nature of the day our visitor sign-in requirements will be somewhat relaxed."

Résumés

Résumés can be useful in your quest to undermine the company, or specific individuals within the company. You're sure to find some as you snoop around in those file cabinets and drawers. If you're targeting a specific individual for gaslighting or firing, a résumé offers crucial information on that person's professional career, and possibly some personal information as well. It may show other offices within the same company that the person worked for or in. So you should target those files next to gather data about your target guinea pig.

Embarrassing Internal Memos

Fax out embarrassing memos to the news media (see Media Maneuvers above), to clients and customers, or to employees — whomever is most affected by the memo. In a large New York ad agency I found a communiqué discussing "creative financial techniques" that would cheat actors out of payments due them for acting in a TV commercial. Since the actors were local talent and not SAG contractees, it was unlikely they understood their rights; furthermore, the agency held off informing the actors exactly who among them were featured in the commercial and who was cut, thus for a time they were kept in the dark about how much money was due them, and in fact the actors would be denied a $13,700 payment by the agency's creative management. Naturally these memos were all marked CONFIDENTIAL. How would those naïve natives feel if they were given a peek at those letters? Outraged, I'm sure, and I've a feeling these sort of shady practices are commonplace in the ad game.

I'm reminded of the case of Katz Radio Group in New York, who was the subject of humiliating embarrassment, boycotts, and anger, when an internal strategy document was released that discouraged corporations from dealing with minority radio stations. "Advertisers should want prospects, not suspects," read the memo.[5] If you're particularly evil, first send a copy of the memo to all the bigwigs at the company, saying you'll take money to keep it hush-hush. Give them enough time to worry, but not enough time to actually plan any counterstrikes and then fax out the memos to the media.

As you can see there are all kinds of important files, papers, and forms you might come across. Files from almost any office can be valuable in some way, although some offices might be more valuable than others. Some companies have a "problem hotline," for instance, where workers can call in to report concerns or to whistle-blow. If you can track down the office where this is run you're sure to find stuff to make your hair stand on end. But any office is gonna have something or other to use. The most important papers you could either steal or run through the shredder. For some really important papers they might have to go to the trouble of hiring a temp or someone to replace the missing documents. They might even fire the person who "lost" the papers in the first place! All that of course will keep the company off-track and away from performing money-making work.

Attack #46. Trip Up Their Telephones

When the General Accounting Office reported on the USDA's telephone usage in 1996, they found so much fraud and unwholesomeness going on that you might find it worthwhile to take USDA employees as your mentors as you force your target company to go out of business. Do what the USDA did: Place lots of long distance calls, especially overseas, and especially to costly adult chat lines if you can get away with it. Accept 1,200 collect calls in four months, and if you can, patch the calls through to long distance numbers (some phone systems let you transfer a call to a number outside the company). Of course we mustn't blame the USDA for the hackers who infiltrated their phone system and made between $40,000 and $50,000 worth of international long distance calls at their expense. As you rummage through files in your espionage activities, perhaps you too will find the PINs and passwords needed to pull off a monumental stunt like that. GAO released similar figures for the DEA (Drug Enforcement Administration) who also apparently don't review their phone bills, for in a year and half more than $2 million was paid to phone companies for fraudulent calls made by phone hackers.[6] Too bad it's our tax money paying for all that.

Now just think if you could put the power of the telephone to work for you against the company you wish to go out of business!

Someone or other should still have the manuals that came with the phone system. Pore over them carefully for instructions on how to mess up their lives. For example, you can set up customer service and sales phones to transfer directly into an unused voice mail account.

Through your internal rummaging around you're sure to discover many voice mail codes written down in desk plans and on calendars and elsewhere. You can start accessing their private voice mail messages. One sales rep used this technique on the company he had just left. He took a new job at a competing firm, but since he still knew how to access his former company's voice mail, he kept checking it to listen to confidential messages about leads and competitive bids so he would have the upper hand when dealing with potential clients.[7]

Small companies have an answering machine or two that picks up. Find the manual nearby. Find out if there is a way to access the machine remotely, and what the code numbers are to do so. Then you can call up and listen in to their messages. You can use these tricks on voice mail boxes and answering machines too:

- Erase messages from customers wishing to place orders.

- Call back customers with problems, impersonating a member of the company, and do a real lousy job of customer disservice.

- Leave your own messages on their answering machine or voice mail, pretending to be current customers saying they've had enough and wish to cancel their subscription or return the product.

- Erase or change the greeting that customers hear when they phone in and the answering machine or voice mail picks up. You could change the greeting to say the company has gone out of business, and customers should call Rival Corp about their services. Or you can say the company will be closed for a month, so don't call back till then. Any change to their message will cause some headaches for the firm.

- When you're done, change the PIN code so they are locked out of their own answering machine or voice mail.

Attack #47. Prick Them With Their Pins

Looking through desks you'll find pins with the company logo on them (to lend an air of authenticity when breaking in to the building or at trade shows) as well as badges, or the magnetic card from inside a badge. If someone is away on vacation they might've left it behind. You might also find other uniforms or accessories, such as trade show shirts, patches or iron-ons with the company logo, that can be used for "disguises." This might not be enough to convince a company employee you work for them, but it may convince a rival. Let's say you stroll into a trade show wearing a corporate pin. Sashay over to their rival's booth and start innocently revealing information about the company, making threats, or provoking arguments. You might also visit the booths of companies who do business with your target firm, or who are clients of your firm. If you can convince them that you work for the company, you can lead them astray in all sorts of ways, such as promising what can't be delivered, or extracting sensitive information from them about the deal they've got going with the company.

Attack #48. The Makings of a Forgery

Take samples of all the stationery, envelopes, and mailing labels you find, for use in forgeries. Take interoffice (intracompany) envelopes with the company logo and address on it, to use for effective in-house forgeries. Some people use a particular kind of PostIt or sticky note (like with a funny picture or joke on it). By using a similar pad you can falsify notes from that person. Annual reports are a public source where forge-worthy signatures can often be found. Now that you've got the stuff, here are some ideas for pranks to pull:

- Falsify a letter from an executive to lower ranks detailing some new policies that everyone is sure to hate. "Everyone is expected to show up one hour earlier once a month for periodic urine testing. Naturally because this is a health issue, fees for these inspections will be taken from your paychecks." (You can go one better than this. After distributing a phony letter like this, plant clues so everyone will suspect a certain company insider as the letter-writer.)

- Put in requests for meaningless busywork to be done. For instance, a note from an executive to his assistant: "Janet — please make three copies of expense records for the past three years, and deliver to Jenkins, Matheson, and Kirkland."

- Or the contrary: Send a note from a higher-up boss asking that certain daily or weekly routines be discontinued. The lower-down boss will be left wondering why the work isn't coming in any more. He won't realize that "his boss requested it."

- After looking through their paper file cabinets, find the biggest, thickest, orneriest folder crammed full of pages going back to the Ice Age. Then leave a request on someone's desk requesting a photocopy of a particular paper in that file. Of course the paper doesn't exist.

- Write and send out whistle-blowing letters to various media organizations and activist groups, exposing the company's secret vices.

All these pranks are sure to cause friction, increase suspicions, and waste much time in that bad old company of yours. Believe it or not, this sort of thing goes on in real life too. As recently as 1988, a representative at a large advertising agency responded to a distraught consumer letter by writing back several racially offensive and insulting replies.[8] Of course the offensive letters were shown around with shock to various organizations, and sent off to clients of the agency, and as word got around the ad agency feared it would lose its clients to the scandal. They did lose one client, and the agency representative who'd written the missives was fired, and an awful lot of sweat poured out over an incident that shouldn't have happened in the first place. But it did. And if your company is too smart to behave as irresponsibly as that one, maybe you'll have to help them along.

Attack #49. Useful Forms

Bureaucracies revel in forms, and forms can be the business-destroyer's best friend. After all, if you fill out a form neatly and submit it to the proper department, chances are it will be acted upon without a moment's hesitation. It's just a matter of finding the forms, knowing how to fill them out, whose signature to forge, and how to submit them. And since businesses use lots and lots of forms, you'll have plenty of filled-out forms all laid out for your study and scrutiny.

- **Temp requisition forms.** Set up a scam whereby you or a pal requisitions a temp for a non-existent absent employee.

- **The phantom employee con.** Scam investigator Chuck Whitlock reports that con artists have opened bank accounts under phony names, then infiltrated a company's payroll system, adding the fictitious names to the payroll, and having their paychecks direct-deposited into those accounts.[9]

- **Federal Express forms** have routing stickers that can be removed or jumbled around to cause trouble. Or simply send many heavy packages out of the company using the company's FedEx ID number.

- **Employees who deal with the public** (customer service/tech support) may have product request forms which they use to send replacement parts or products to customers. Make sure you send out wrong or incompatible pieces or products to customers who won't understand why they're receiving them and will call in to complain about it.

Out of Business
Force a company, business, or store to close its doors...
for good!
152

- **Post private employee evaluation forms in public.** Or fill in the information to make up some damaging stuff and put them on file or in public.

- **Cancellation forms.** If your company provides a service or subscription, perhaps you can find cancellation forms laying around. Make plenty of photocopies and give them out at every opportunity. You want to make it easy for customers to deregister, cancel, null and void their contracts for good. Some computer companies might be listed at **www.cancel-it.com** which makes it easy to cancel certain computing services on-line.

In the files of one very efficient executive secretary I found a two-page document explaining everything a replacement secretary has to do to prepare travel arrangements for the big bosses. Included was this enlightening snippet:

"There are samples in the credenza of how to fill out the AMEX cash advance form where I keep the forms (top drawer, right hand side). Ted will have to sign the AMEX cash advance form in 3 places I believe. Put "Sign Here" stickies by each place he needs to sign the advance. Ask him for his AMEX card. Bring his card along with the cash advance form upstairs to the credit union. They'll give you the money. Double check it. Give Ted the money and his AMEX card. Put the AMEX receipt in the brown voucher pocket folder (upper left hand shelf in the sliding door cabinet by my desk)."

Once you learn internal procedures, it won't be hard to get things rolling in your direction. And wouldn't you like a cash advance off the big boss's American Express card! If nothing else you've learned where all the credit card forms are filed, off which you can probably get enough information to make the executive's life miserable for a while. The hard part of this will be getting the boss's credit card. (See Tail the Mail, Attack #27 for one idea.)

You've probably noticed that by rummaging through desks you will accumulate a lot of information (photos, Rolodexes, business cards, notes, files, and more papers galore). And there are a lot of mischievous ways for you to use that information. If it seems like too much, don't let it overwhelm you. I'm not saying you should do all this stuff in one shot (although you may have to if you can't get back inside the company). I'm talking about gathering such information slowly, one office at a time. Many different people can be involved in doing different offices. Many people can do the same low-risk areas like copy rooms, taking turns swiping faxes that have been left behind, or taking turns rummaging in certain trash bins, etc. Not necessarily a one-person job. You can gather more info and more complete info, safer, by using teams of people (not just yourself). One example is to have one person who befriends the security guards, asks them a lot of questions, but a completely different person makes use of that information. The two people may pretend not to know each other, and in fact the two people might never visibly be friends in the eyes of the company. One person might work as a temp one week, talking and gathering information, then the next week an intern starts up who makes use of that info. The connection is not made between the two people.

Citations

1. Rosenbluth, Hal F. and Diane McFerrin. *The Customer Always Comes Second: And Other Secrets of Exceptional Service.* pp. 30-31.
2. Greenberg. His memos on watching expenses can be found throughout the book.
3. Washington Researchers Publishing, *How Competitors Learn Your Company's Secrets.* p. 13.
4. "Inside Track: You Don't Have to Be Agent 007 to Benefit From Competitive Intelligence," in *Entrepreneur.* February 1996. pp 86-87. Article uprighteously advocating some legal means of industrial espionage.
5. Pristin, Terry. "Radio Ad Marketer Apologizes for Memo Offending Minorities" in *The New York Times.* Saturday, May 16, 1998. p. B3. Article about a company whose racist internal memo was leaked to the media — and the uproar it caused.
6. Wenman, Cosmo. "Party Lines: How the Government Calls on Your Dime" in *Reason.* October 1996. p. 16. Short article on fraudulent calls in the USDA and DEA.
7. Dellecave, Jr., Tom. "Insecurity Is Techology Putting Your Company's Primary Asset — Its Information — At Risk!, in *Sales & Marketing Management.* April 1996. p. 40.
8. Hendon, Donald. *Classic Failures in Product Marketing: Market Principle Violations and How to Avoid Them.* NTC Business Books. p. 24.
9. Whitlock, Chuck. *Chuck Whitlock's Scam School.* MacMillan. New York. p. 141.

Special Tactic Report: Piecing Together Evidence

The more industrial espionage you engage in, the more likely it is you'll run across shredded documents that you *really wish* you could read. Let's take some time then to discuss some methods of piecing together evidence.

Start off by breaking their shredder machine so they can't use it in the first place. It will make all the rest of this unnecessary.

Now a lot of times companies don't have a shredder. They merely rip up papers by hand. This is never effective. I remember one of my bosses once instructing me on how to dispose of confidential documents: "Tear up the paper into six pieces, like this," she said, showing me how — as if six pieces would deter the determined spy.

To restore torn or shredded papers, choose a well-lighted work area that won't be disturbed with breezes — no door to suddenly fly open and stir up a wind, else all those paper scraps will go flying. You need a roll of not too sticky transparent tape, or masking tape, and preferably the tape should be in one of those weighted desk dispensers so you can use one hand.

Start by sorting the papers. An article in *2600* advises, "There are so many differences in the angle of each shred, what text each document contained, which color its paper was, and which weight, that the identification of individual documents by their shreds is fairly simple."[1] You can discard pieces that are blank on both sides if you only really care about reading what was on the pages.

If you notice any stacks of papers while sorting, try to keep those together because they are probably from the same batch of sheets. If you see stacks where the top pieces are ragged to the right, bottom pieces ragged to the left, you can figure the top half of the stack was probably at one point joined to the bottom half. The person shredding merely tore the stack in half, stacked one half on top of the other, and threw it in the waste receptacle. A common paper tearing pattern is ABAB. The paper is torn in half, and one half is put under the other. Then torn in half the other direction, and again stacked up, and thus the ABAB pattern is formed. If you're piecing together scraps that a human ripped up, the task is not too difficult. It's just like a jigsaw puzzle. As you match pieces together, hold them in place with a little tape.

But if you're piecing together shredded pages, it becomes more time consuming. One tip from the *2600* article[2] is to use masking tape to place down a strip on an oversized board. Pick up another, see if it matches. If not, place it down elsewhere on the board far away. As you pick up more and more pieces, eventually some will start to match up, and as they do, you begin to have less and less choices as to where to place the strips (in other words, the further you proceed, the better you get at the game because there are less wrong moves to make). As you start grouping strips together in correct match-ups, you can start moving around groups of strips together to complete whole pages.

He also mentions that if you suspect it's a shredded form (like an order form), try to get the whole form[3] so you can compare your progress to the real thing — sort of like seeing the completed picture on the cover of a jigsaw puzzle box. In some cases it won't be necessary to go through the entire mending process. If you only care about being able to read the data, you can probably make do with a partial reconstruction, but be careful because you might misinterpret what things say if you don't have the whole picture. If a row of numbers is cut off at the bottom, for instance, you might mistake the top of a 7 for a 3. A point could be the top of a 4 or a 1.

If you get real good at this you can get yourself a job at the Office of Currency Standards in Washington, D.C. They're the people who piece together damaged money people send to them using straight pins, knitting needles, tape, tweezers, and magnifying glasses. They unshred money that's been torn, burned, buried, laundered, eaten by pets, and exposed to chemicals.[4] If you get discouraged while piecing together the papers you found, just remember, someone out there has it worse — someone is piecing together money that's recently passed through a golden retriever's bowels.

> **Out of Business**
> Force a company, business, or store to close its doors...
> for good!
> 158

Citations

1. Fluvius, Datum. "Unshredding the Evidence" in *2600 Magazine*. Spring 1996. p. 10. Offers tips on putting back together pages that have gone through a "spaghetti shredder."
2. *Ibid.*, p. 10.
3. *Ibid.*, p. 11.
4. Weber, Bruce. "No Money in the Microwave, Please" in *The New York Times Magazine*. December 10, 1989. p. 126. Article on the O.C.S., the Office of Currency Standards which pieces together damaged paper money.

An Employee's Computer

Computers are ubiquitous, necessary, and expensive, hence swell targets for attack. The Gartner Group did a survey that estimated companies pay $7,700 per year per Windows 95 or NT desktop, and about $8,800 for the average Windows 3.1 desktop. Costs included training, tech support, repair and maintenance, and the like.[1] These numbers sound a little inflated, but even the lowball figure is much more than the average computer is selling for nowadays. With your help, I'm sure we can punch those dollar amounts every skyward.

Attack #50. Computers — Unplugged

It's easier to be destructive than constructive. That fact helps you out immensely, for what you can destroy in mere seconds or minutes, will take hours to repair. Sneak into the place with a good pair of wire cutters and screwdrivers, and get to work.

- Switch around plugs. Attach the highly-sensitive main server computers to an outlet controlled by the kitchen light switch, or some other switch that is often shut off.

- Mess up their printer. Take a pair of needle nose pliers. Unplug the printer cable that runs from the printer to the computer. The end of the cable is filled with little metallic pins. Break off some of the pins with the pliers, then re-connect the cable. (Make sure you throw away the broken pins!) Now data can't flow through the cable properly. The printer won't work and they'll go crazy trying to figure out why. This leads to frustration, downtime, and money spent on printer repairs or a new printer.

- Plug their expensive computer equipment directly into the walls, removing any surge protectors they have in place. No one will notice them gone, and even if they do they'll think the MIS (Management Information System) department took them. Now if lightning strikes or there's a power surge — ZAP!

- Tamper with their uninterruptible power supplies. A UPS is a system that keeps the electricity flowing smoothly even when the power goes out or there are powerful surges of current on the line, thus preventing computer crashes and associated problems. At one company where a UPS was used on major systems (but not on minor systems), the crash of the "minor" systems cost more than $1,000 to piece back together.[2] So see if you can disable these things, then stand back and let Mother Nature do your dirty work for you.

- Steal mouse balls. Cut the cords too, while you're at it. Mouse cords, keyboard cords, anything that connects one thing to another — slice it!

The best computers to attack are the servers. Those are the main computers where data is stored. E-mail and internet systems often work off the servers, so if you can take down those machines the company will be severely crippled. Consider the story of VMEbus International Trade Association which was constantly bombarded with phone calls. "We'd get calls while we were on calls, and then we'd have to call everyone back. Our day was a constant, incessantly interrupted by the phone," complained executive director Ray Alderman. Sounds like a bad situation, right? Poor customer service, frenzied, overworked employees, and to top it off, their phone bill was $1,500 per month. Alderman's point in telling the story was that when they set up a web page with frequently asked questions, their phone bill dropped to less than $500 a month, and presumably the workload became more manageable and relaxed. Now the moral of this story should be clear: If you can reverse the procedure, you can cause the opposite result. Remember, it's easier to destroy than to build.

Attack #51. Web Browsers

Web browsers may hold secrets that individual users would not care to be divulged. Start by looking at the bookmark list. This is a list of special internet sites the user has specifically bookmarked as being important. What do you find there? Nudie stuff? Job search materials? Write it down in your Revenge List. Access to the company directory? Needed reference materials? Un-mark those bookmarks to make access to information harder for that employee.

Cache files are another way to spy on where a user has been. Microsoft Internet Explorer saves cache in different spots. Windows 95 version uses C:\Windows\Temporary Internet Files. You can also look in the **cache** and **history** directories to see clues. Look at the time/date stamps when files were created to see if sites were visited during work hours.

Even if you don't find anything seamy going on, you can make something seamy happen. Rig up their web browsers to actively seek out pornographic sites. For instance most web browsers allow you to designate a home page and a search page. Wouldn't it be funny if every time he boots up his browser, it goes to the home page of Double Dick Dan The Two Dicked Man? Or whenever he clicks on the search button, it brings him to Aunt Annie's Tales of Inter-Familial Anal Fun? (To change these pages in Netscape 3.0, click on **Options > General Preferences > Appearance**. Click on **Home Page Location**, and in the **Browser Starts With** field, type the web address of the new home page. In Microsoft Internet Explorer 3.0 click on **View > Options > Navigation**. There you can define the start page, search page, and five "Quick Links.")

You can also use their computers to actively seek out pornographic web sites and start downloading dirty pictures (and video, and whatever else you can come up with). Hope that the company's thought police will be monitoring such activity and not take too kindly to it. Of course the person whose computer it is will deny vehemently that he ever visited such web sites, but his denials will only make the case against him look stronger.

Attack #52. Scheduling Programs

Computer scheduling programs such as Microsoft's Schedule+ reveal all about an executive's day. Also look for calendars and paper organizers. You can also find out about routines (every day they eat lunch someplace or go to the gym) or personal appointments like doctor or car (external factors that can be intercepted). If you know about a meeting in advance, you will be able to infiltrate it later, or at the very least you'll know this guy's office will be empty at that time. You might find an alarm has been set to remind him to go to his appointment 15 minutes before. (Are the other meetings also alarmed in this way? If it's the only one, maybe that's a more important meeting.) Try to tie up their time by scheduling in false phone calls that they will prepare for and wait for, but never come. Change the time of get-togethers slightly so the executive shows up 30 minutes late (but thinks he's right on time), or shows up dressed for a golf outing when really it's a formal conference. And of course you can really screw up a vice president or someone by erasing important meetings from their schedule altogether. And don't forget to erase them from their assistant's and secretary's computers too so absolutely no one will remember the important date.

Attack #53. Customer Lists

You may find spreadsheets, database files, or even word processor documents containing customer names and contact information.

Now that you've got em, what to do with them?

Start by making significant changes to the customer lists you discover. Change billing data so the company will send out invoices for less money than they're supposed to be billing. Make subtle changes to addresses so they send those invoices to the wrong office or floor. Introduce misspellings into the first and last names of conceited customers who will be extremely offended that their names have been misspelled. Any name that ends with -sky change to -ski, and vice versa. Convert Juniors to Seniors. Use nicknames instead of the full name spelled out. Little things can be quite offensive to some people.

Now, after you're finished messing everything up, you'll want to grab all those customer lists you find, copy them onto floppy disks and bring them home with you. There are several fiendish ways to (mis)use the customer lists you come across.

If you run a rival business you'll want to use this inside info to figure out what the customers are getting from *them* that you can provide cheaper, faster, better, or with more flair. If you don't run a rival business the lists might still somehow be mailed to all the company's competitors, not that you would do anything like that yourself of course. Or simply let the customers know that other customers are getting the same, or similar products or services cheaper from the same company.

Business consultant Piyush Patel suggests cold calling new customers and asking suspicious questions like, "Has the product crashed yet? Did you lose your data?" Explain that everything was going well until a few months after using their product, when it started failing. As the situation became worse and worse, the company started getting less and less responsive, until finally they had to stop using the product. Start planting fears like that in customers' heads and they'll treat any little tremor as a major earthquake — and woe be the company if a major earthquake really does strike.

Some customer lists will be part of a call tracking system. Companies often have a customer service or technical support center devoted to dealing with customers over the phone. Customer Service Representatives (CSRs) log those calls into a database to keep a history on each customer. The intent is to provide better customer service, but that can backfire on them too, especially if they've got you adding nasty comments in the system. A bulletin aimed at customer service managers warns:

> ...what a CSR logs in the database about a customer can severely impact the level of service that customer receives. For example, what if your CSR enters "constant complainer," "frequent returns" or "old grouch" in a customer's files? Accurate or not, won't the next CSR who assists that customer treat the customer differently because of these comments?

> In worst case scenarios, companies have faced lawsuits by entering sensitive information in customer databases that was later proven to discriminate against customers in violation of the law. Others have faced sabotage by disgruntled employees who deliberately enter false information in the databases.[3]

It's even better if customers have access to their call history as well. At one workplace I encountered a customer ranting and raving because she had read the statements made about her on the company's computer system. The statements included some rather harsh words from one employee who meant them as an inside joke — he didn't realize the joke was open for anyone with a computer to see. There went one unhappy customer out the door, and who knows how many more she dragged with her.

Another way to foul up customer lists is by adding extra records that will make good customers appear bad. For instance you could add false returns to a good customer's record in the database. That customer will be seen as suspicious; why do they keep ordering products and then returning them? Certain products, like computer software, may restrict customers to a licensing agreement, and it may be possible to show the customer has violated that agreement by requesting multiple extensions and installations of the software well beyond the original contract. The next time the customer calls in with a legitimate request, these false records will make customer service representatives respond with accusations and suspicion, causing tempers to flare in the hearts of loyal customers.

Customer lists come in many forms, and come about for many reasons. In the offices of top execs you might find account profiles, or packages put together to brief the executive on who he's likely to encounter at a meeting or party he's attending. From these you can find out who the top clients are, key points about the relationship between the company and that client, and personal data about the client that can be used in your attacks. One briefing I found gave 15 pages of top executives, their phones and addresses, spouse's name and other personal information, annual revenue the client makes for the company, any recent problems with the customer, obstacles and issues of concern, competitive activity, summary of overall relationship with the customer, goals and strategies for dealing with that customer, and pending sales. Here's a document less than 20 pages that gives so much valuable information that if it found its way into the wrong hands the damage would be unthinkable — and it was all to prepare a V.P. for a cocktail party!

Attack #54. Information Gathered From Software

You can find out some useful information poking about in the software on a person's computer. If you click on the **File** menu of most word processors and spreadsheets you can see their recently used file list (the list of documents the users have been editing most recently), which tells you what's important to them at the moment. If you go to the About box (usually **Help > About**) you may find a serial number or registration number for the software. This can be used for various scams. For example, if the software company offers paid-for technical support, call them, offer the serial number you found, and ask to be billed to the corporate account. Now you can get all your questions answered, unknown to them, at the company's expense.

It's also handy to look for stuck jobs. Print jobs that have "errored out" and are stuck in the Print Manager, for instance. If you're in after hours at night you may find that something didn't get printed out as they thought it did. Also check to see if there is paper in the fax and printer. You may find a present comes out for you. Also you can send huge print jobs to the printer from everyone's computer. When they come in next morning they'll find that all their computers are busy spitting

out page after page to the printer, and most of them won't
have a clue how to shut it off.

Finally, consider the fact that most businesses nowadays
rely extensively on information of some kind or another, and
maybe you can find a way to stop up the flow of information
they're used to relying upon. For instance, the company relies
on access to certain kinds of databases, stock information, or
industry reports. Construction companies may pick up new
business by reading reports of new building projects and putting in bids on the projects that interest them. Find their source
of data and stop it up — and you'll be helping to stop their
business from growing any more.

Attack #55. E-Mail Evil

E-Mail is often stored in a folder or directory called "Sent"
or "Outgoing" after it is sent. Look in the outgoing electronic
mailbox for confidential messages. Common e-mail packages
like Lotus Notes, Eudora, Netscape Communicator, and really
any e-mail program store all messages that have been sent and
received unless the user specifically deletes them. Most people
don't realize everything is stored there and so easily accessible. Take this example of an e-mail I found in an executive's
computer. He was writing about a particularly huge client of
theirs:

> The [client's] status is not particularly good right
> now. I've never had trouble convincing a customer of
> the value of our parts over [rival's], particularly in
> this area. These guys seem to have already made their
> minds up to go with [rival] and seem to be ignoring

> or discounting as hype any technical/architectural arguments. I feel that our best hope is to have [rival] fail during on-premises trials. Even then, it would probably have to be a pretty big failure for the people at [client] to admit that they made a poor recommendation to their upper management.... I don't know of anything else that you, or I, or the account team could do now that is not already in the works.

A message like this might paint the company in a bad light. If some failure did occur and this message was leaked, the company might be blamed for the problem. You might also find (or plant) evidence of e-mailing away company secrets. You could frame someone by sending out e-mails from their e-mail address that contains confidential files or reports.

Forge Their Signature

Another way to cause problems is to create for them a damaging signature file. A signature is a file that contains a few lines of text that gets appended to the bottom of e-mail messages and news postings that the user sends. The e-mail software does this automatically. It's usually used by people to automatically attach a tagline about their business, or a favorite quote or song lyric, to the bottom of messages they send. But if used improperly it can cause embarrassment. What if you set up a signature that reads, "Employee for sale to highest bidder...Have a job offer? I'll take it! I'm looking to get out of this place." Or one that gives away some crucial trade secrets. Every time they send a message, the signature will be attached to the bottom and they won't even realize it. You would want to do this mostly for employees who send messages to people outside the company, for instance, to customers and prospective customers. Different e-mail software have different means of editing the signature.

A final e-mail attack is to sign up key employees to mailing lists and junk mail lists. For many employees it is crucial they check their e-mail constantly, for many important messages are sent to them. If they were to suddenly start receiving dozens or hundreds of messages, the important messages would get lost in the shuffle. It would be quite annoying too. You can sign up people to electronic mailing lists. One way is to use Yahoo to find them. Go to **www.yahoo.com** then search for the keywords "mailing lists." You will be presented with a list of all sorts of categories of mailing lists, start clicking links and you'll find dozens upon dozens of mailing lists to which you can subscribe your unsuspecting turkeys. My favorite is the Libertarian list which seems to put out an ungodly number of posts each day.

Attack #56. Perpetrate Macros and Disable Viral Detection

What your company really needs to help it out of business is a deadly disease — like a virus. A computer virus, I mean. How damaging can these things be to a business? An investigation by AT&T Corporate Security counted 600 confirmed cases of viruses, and perhaps twice as many cases that went unreported, with workers suffering over 3,000 lost working hours due to computer down-time.[4]

See what virus detection software is in effect. If it's old there may be a new virus that it doesn't catch. Check with local computer gurus who know such stuff. You can probably deactivate the software without anyone noticing. For instance, in Windows 95 and Windows 98 click on **Start > Settings > Taskbar > Start Menu Programs > Remove**. Scroll down to the **Startup** folder, and double-click on **Startup**. If you see any virus-detection software (like Norton AntiVirus or McAfee) click on it so it's highlighted, then click the **Remove** button to remove it. The next time the computer is rebooted, the scanning software won't load automatically. (For some virus detection software it may be necessary to edit AUTO-EXEC.BAT or the CONFIG.SYS files.) Some word processors now include virus protection to protect against macro viruses. This too you'll want to deactivate. Most users won't realize they're not protected anymore.

■ **www2.spidernet.net/web/~cvrl//** Computer Virus Research Lab sells CD-ROMs with over 13,000 live virii. Plus they have links to other virus sites.

■ **www.antionline.com/archives/virii** Another massive catalog of virii. These are directly downloadable, but must be compiled first before they can be used.

■ **www.notme.ncsa.uiuc.edu/people/ncsairst/ERS-SVA-E01-1997:003.1** This site is run by the International Computer Security Association to alert you to all the different hoax viruses out there — and give you ideas on creating your own, I imagine.

Attack #57. Unsettle Their Settings

Computers have tons of settings that must be set exactly right, or little things will start to go wrong here and there.

You can disable the energy-saving features of monitors and computers. It is estimated that the Energy Star system saves

$35 or more a year,[5] so be sure to go into the Control Panel and disable it all because we want wasteful spendings, not savings. In the Control Panel you can also remove their modem, or reinstall it as a completely different modem than the one they actually have, which will cause them weird problems when they try to dial out on-line. Selecting the wrong video driver might leave them working fine awhile — until the monitor blows out.

Alter the custom dictionaries in word processors. Most word processors have a custom dictionary file that contains words not found in the main dictionary that installs with the software. Say Robert Smellfist works for Jack Mioff Enterprises. He might add "Smellfist" and "Mioff" to the custom dictionary so the computer recognizes the correct spelling of those names. You, however, have sneaked in and changed the spellings, and added your own misspellings to the dictionary, so every time Robert spell-checks a document, it comes out filled with errors which Robert, being the corporate drone he is, is too dumb to notice. Try to do this in advertising and public relations departments where snafus will be seen outside the company as well as causing headaches inside.

Networking and Internet settings are incredibly difficult to get right, and can cause major downtime and loss of productivity. Besides that, they require specially-trained technicians to repair. For example, in Microsoft Internet Explorer 3.0, select **View > Options** and you'll be presented with several panels of preferences that can be maliciously destroyed, and security settings that can be disabled. In Netscape 3.0 there are lots and lots of settings that are difficult to get set up right. Even minor changes (changing an "m" to an "n" or removing a hyphen, or adding a period) on **Options > Mail and News Pref-**

erences > **Servers** will mess things up. Go down the **Options** menu, selecting all the different **Preferences** screens, flicking your spray of harmful wreckage every which way you can.

Attack #58. Billing Systems

Money makes the business world go round. Find a way to stop their money coming in, and the business comes crashing to a halt. Check out this angry missive:

Medicare
Attn: Ms Chopstick
FAX: 888-555-1234

Dear Sirs:

As per our conversation with Ms. Chopstick today, I am faxing you my request for an address change for Dr. Palo Alto and Dr. San Juan from 66 Old Town Road, to 2 Snow Court. Please note that I have <u>twice</u> before requested this change in writing and I just found out that our address has not been changed because many Medicare checks were sent to 66 Old Town Road (the address of our former office) and that the practice currently there accidentally deposited the checks into their account. We have many more Medicare claims filed, and if our address is not changed in an expeditious fashion, the checks will continue to go to the wrong address. We therefore request that our address be corrected as promptly as possible. Thank you for your attention to this matter.

Yours truly
Dr. Palo Alto
Dr. San Juan

P.S. I am also faxing you a copy of one of the forms that I previously sent to you, just for your records. Please note the date.

Think of all the trouble, aggravation, and lost revenue this screw-up caused this medical practice. Now think of all the screwups you can cause for your own targeted company. What if you started intentionally putting in change-of-address forms for your business, so the insurance companies or whomever sends in the checks start sending them to the wrong address? You can also see if their computerized billing system can be stopped in some way. For instance, can the computer be re-programmed with new codes or numbers so as to write bills for slightly lesser amounts? Or perhaps an address can be subtly changed on outgoing bills so incoming mail will be delayed or misrouted.

The doctors at this same practice, in a highly competitive field, discovered one day their billing system had stopped working shortly after taking on a new peer. They suspected she had "done something to it" unintentionally, but nevertheless they found they hadn't been getting any money in because the system was broken and bills weren't being sent to insurance companies. To make matters worse, they later found out that the new doctor didn't know how to bill, or didn't know everything that was billable so she did lots of work without collecting money for it. This could've gone on forever if someone hadn't caught it. One of the big causes of business failure is an inadequate understanding of accounting, but in this technological age we can add that the knowledge of technology is crucial as well.

Attack #59. Boxed Disks Massacres

Computer disks in boxes might be backups, or you might find CD-ROMs of useful information. Some companies now keep confidential financial records or travel and entertainment records on CD-ROM which may be useful in various ways. In any case, it's a lot easier to pocket a little CD and walk off with it, than it is to walk away with a whole file cabinet full of information. Technology makes espionage so much easier. If you find boxes of blank disks, wouldn't it be fun to plant viruses on them? Users naturally trust a blank disk straight out of the box, so would not feel obligated to scan for viruses. It usually takes a few months or more to go through a box of blank disks, which means that you would be wreaking havoc on their precious data for many months or years to come.

Attack #60. Computer Files

Résumé on their hard drive? That implies they're secretly plotting to leave. Maybe that person could become an ally in your quest against the company. Or perhaps you find embarrassing graphical images or pornographic stories on their computers. You might find presentations that show the company's business strategies or marketing plans. Business strategies fail as often as they work (or fail more often), so just knowing them strikes the balance in your favor. PublishIt! and other publishing programs might show you new box designs or ad layouts. Delete the files and they'll be forced to redo their whole ad campaign from scratch.

Also look for job description files, "desk plans," and files that give overviews of the job and info for temps and interns. These sorts of files often divulge voice mail passwords, internal procedures, and computer passwords.

TMP files may be left behind from crashed or failed jobs, and may hold fragments of long-deleted documents. They may also give you access to data which would otherwise be pass-word protected. TMP files can be loaded into any word processor to see if they hold treasure or garbage.

Look through all word processing documents (business correspondence and e-mail) and spreadsheets. A friend of mine found a spreadsheet containing all of his co-workers' salaries and other useful bargaining chips on his boss's computer. Certainly you could use such data to spread rebellion and bitterness throughout the ranks.

Look for mathematical models (such as spreadsheets with calculations in it) that they use frequently (or infrequently even) without much thought, just plugging in numbers. Make slight changes to make the numbers work out better than normal.

For instance, at one book company I know of they base buying decisions in part on a Profit & Loss statement which is a spreadsheet that calculates potential profits of a book. To use it, a lowly editorial assistant plugs in some numbers into the spreadsheet which calculates percentages that are used to make the buying decisions. If the numbers were cranked up slightly higher, the company would begin to make a series of poor buying decisions (as far as the numbers can be trusted to be effective determinants of sales). Even just a few poor decisions can have a ripple-down effect.

Often you'll find a document like the following one on an employee's computer. You might have to read between the lines a little to get some use out of it. Here is the document on the left, and my comments on the right.

Jamie's stuff — in no particular order —
4/26

KEN —
TOP ACCOUNT LISTS
MASS MARKET

The computer disk for the top accounts and the customer account profile is in the file box on the file cabinet in my cubicle. The top accounts file is on Excel with each different type of account on a separate sheet of the same file. The profile form is on the same disk, in a Word file. There is only one form. I've been changing the heading for each different type of account.

Pointer to information also hints there is no backup form. Lose the form — creates extra work.

DAILY SALES REPORT

The instructions for printing the daily sales report backups are on my bulletin board, in the corner closest to the computer monitor. They are labeled "Getting the sales report from the REEDS system." My sign on is "monet3" and my password is "lillys." Note that we have been having a lot of trouble with the printer this report goes to. Ian Farling knows about the problem.

Useful data for sabotage of system. Also that printer would be a good target of sabotage.

TRADE SHOWS

My show file is in the top drawer of the file cabinet in my cubicle. It's in a red file folder. It's on the side towards the bookcase. I've requested exhibit space and also hotel space, and my notes are in the file. I've told all this to Sandra Jameson.

"I've told all this to Sandra Jameson." She is trying to make herself look good. She believes herself to be a hard worker, does too much without getting credit for her good work.

REP MAILING
There is a file on my computer, in Word, called OUTGOING.DOC. It has the format for the labels I use to do the rep mailing. If you put a set of 30 labels to a page into the printer, you will get the labels you need to do the mailing. The labels are set up in box order.

Now you know where to get addresses of all their sales reps. You'll be better able to keep the sales reps from getting crucial information; and keep the sales reps from making sales.

SALES REP LIST
The sales rep list is up-to-date as of 4/22. It's in my computer in a word file called REPS.DOC. Page 1 of the file contains the rep list. The rest of the pages have other information, that does not necessarily need to be distributed.

BILLS/AMEX BILLS/
AND REP EXPENSE REPORTS
I keep copies of these (in the case of AmEx bills and rep expense reports the first page only) in the bottom drawer of the file cabinet in my cubicle in a set of yellow folders. They are alphabetical with a separate file for each rep.

Expense reports with credit card numbers. Photocopies of AmEx bills.

TRADE SHOW CALENDAR
AND EXPENSES
The up-to-date trade show calendar I have been keeping is in my e-mail. The spreadsheet on my computer is in a file called SHOWCOST.XLS. Reminder to whoever does the fall trade shows: Our tables need to be next to the DrumCo tables so that the in-house sales people can work both of them.

Useful to know what trade shows will be attended, for possible infiltration and destruction.

SALES CONFERENCE EXPENSES

I had planned to add the costs of the April sales meeting in the office and then compare them to see how much we really save by doing it in-house. If you continue doing this exercise Dara Groan or Janice will have the costs of the paper products they purchased and the food they ordered. You will need to add in the cost of the rental of the tablecloths and skirts (they are billing us), as well as the hotel costs and the cost of the dinner at Villa Nouva, which will be on Jeanne's AMEX card. What's not in those numbers, and should be considered is the time it takes Janice, Dara, myself, Carlos and the maintenance people to put this together. That's time that could be used for other things.

There's evidence of discontent here, but you have to read between the lines to see it! She feels that she, Janice, Carlos and the data department and maintenance staffs are being made to do extra work that's not accounted for "in numbers." They're doing the work — others get the credit for it.

SIGN ONS

When you turn the computer on my sign on is HARRIET and my password is PSYETH. To get into Lotus Notes my password is PASSWORD. To get into the Marketing System my sign on is MONET3 and my password is LILLYS. To get into Westminister my sign on is MONET3 and my password is WATER. If one of these doesn't work make sure you're in lower case.

Of much value in helping one to break into their computer systems, unlocking all that marketing and sales data.

> PRINTING THE WEEKLY MARKETING REPORTS
> Sign onto the Marketing System (Sign On MONET3 and password LILLYS — note it's lower case only). Hit enter as instructed and type Y to the two questions that follow. Hit enter again. A blank page will print. Scroll down to #4 and hit enter. Scroll down to Custom reports and hit enter. Scroll down to Matt's weekly reports and hit enter. The reports will now automatically print, one at a time. Note that your keyboard and screen will freeze up while Marketing system reports are printing. Complete instructions for printing the weekly report and the Top 100 report are on my bulletin board; the bottom corner closest to the monitor. It's the two sheets of paper under the sheet of paper on getting the sales reports.

Pointer to a source of further procedures and insights.

All the different computer files mentioned here are useful in various ways. Many will be confidential or marked proprietary or for internal use only. Naturally you should mail them out to rivals, print them in a newspaper advertisement, or make photocopies and leave them lying around in the office of someone who's not supposed to have access to them, or frame someone higher up — make it look as though they were selling the information to another corporation.

When engaging in industrial espionage of this sort, you want to start out by making a list of *what specific pieces of information* would be helpful for you to learn about the company and *why* they would be helpful to know. That way you're not shooting wildly in the dark, and you can make a focused effort. Once you know what you're looking for you can start asking, "How can I find out that piece of information?" By focusing like this you focus your energy onto only important stuff. If you're caught, at least it was in the pursuit of useful info — if you're going to take risks, they should be smart risks not stupid ones.

Examples:

> **What I want to know:** When the sales conference is (and where).
>
> **Why I want to know it:** So I can find out who exactly their customers are.
>
> **How to get that info:** Word documents, garbage, insider source...

An anonymous former business consultant writing in *Fortune* told the method of industrial espionage he'd used when bidding for a new client. He had all the lower-rungs at his company phone their friends at competing firms and find out if they were bidding. Then, "If I know I'm up against a boutique that doesn't have computer-systems capability, you can be sure that my pitch [to the potential client] will be that you have to have new information systems to make the strategy work. And oh, by the way, we're the only guys who can do that."[6] You can see two levels of espionage at play here. Firstly, because he was a knowledgeable consultant, he made it his business to know all about competing firms (like whether they have "computer-systems capability" whatever that means). Secondly, he defined the client's problem as a kind that only his firm could solve. He sold the client on the idea that they were a bunch of screws, and he a bunch of screwdrivers that would twist them out of the hole they were in. This kind of strategy works if you are part of a competing company striving to put a rival out of business.

After making a list you can decide priorities. By the way, while investigating these things you'll undoubtedly come across all sorts of other information — the same info you would've come across had you not been organized. But because you're organized you're better able to determine wheat from chaff. Not only that but you're getting all that extra info anyway.

Citations

1. Hogan, Mike. "Money Matters: Hidden PC Costs" in *PC Computing*. March 1997. pp. 40-41. Short article describes how companies spend money on computers after the initial purchase is done.
2. Winkler, Ira. *Corporate Espionage: What it is, Why it is Happening in Your Company, What You Must do About It*. p. 41.
3. Clement Communications Incorporated. "Do You Know What Employees Are Entering In Customer Databases?" in *Customer Service & Retention*. June 1, 1998. p 3. Short article warning managers to keep track of what's being tracked in their customer databases. Source of the info on the perils of call tracking systems.
4. AT&T Security. *The Security Seven: Your Guide to Protecting AT&T's Treasures*. p. 4.
5. Hogan, p. 40.
6. Anonymous. "Confessions of an Ex-Consultant" in *Fortune*. October 14, 1996. p. 110. A former consultant brags

that he's smart and other consultants are stupid. Used for his example of industrial espionage in a bidding situation.

Special Tactic Report: Teaming Up With Others

No matter how dedicated you are to your cause, it can only be helped by teaming up with other like-minded people. You should try to gather as many people as possible to support your cause of overthrowing this terrible corporation. How can you find other people who will help you? Here are some suggestions:

Teaming Up #1: Cultivate an Insider

The best team-members are insiders, employees who work for the company. Do whatever you can to locate dissatisfied employees. Visit restaurants, watering holes, and neighboring businesses nearby to meet employees of the firm. Use the Mental Attacks, Gaslighting, Internal Rumors, and Random Acts of Violence tactics to arouse resentment in some employees. Then they will be more likely to help out in taking the company down. (Don't tell them that's your goal, because they might want to keep their job. Instead, tell them you merely want to get back at their boss.)

Teaming Up #2: Satisfied Employees

Satisfied employees won't help you overthrow the company, but they are useful in other ways. You shouldn't tell them what you're up to, but you use them as a source of information and advice. If they're really goody-two-shoes, they might be useful to create rumors, if you plant the idea in their heads that so-and-so is disloyal to the firm. They will be sure to spread the false gossip.

Teaming Up #3: Former Employees

Former employees might have quit because they couldn't take it, or they might have been fired. Either are fair game in this unfair war. Put ads in the papers or on the Internet, visit bars and restaurants near competing companies, or just use your networking skills to contact people who *used to work there,* but now don't. At one company I found a pissed-off letter from the company president to the unemployment office pleading with them not to allow a former employee unemployment benefits because of the animosity generated between him and her. That former employee might be the perfect gal to have on your team. In another office I found this letter which also hints at dark goings ons:

Mrs. Penny Smith
121 Dackmarrow Street
Orange, CA 90211

re: Employment at Crown Enterprises

Dear Penny:

This letter is in reference to the conversation we had today concerning your employment at our office. You asked us if you could work for us again, but change your status from full-time to part-time employment. This would imply that you no longer work for us; however, we never notified you that you don't work here any more and we still consider you a full-time employee. We understand that you missed a lot of work due to your son's illness, and I believe that we have been extremely fair and flexible with you, considering the amount of time you have missed in your first few months of work. In fact, we thought that you might have quit, since you stopped coming to work almost four weeks ago and we had not heard from you in almost two weeks. However, as I previously mentioned, the full-time job is still yours. We can not, however, keep it vacant any longer. We expect you to report to our office for full-time employment on Monday, March 5 at 10:00 AM, if you wish to continue in our employment.

Yours truly,

Ruth

Your espionage activity will almost certainly come up with some leads to former employees such as this one who may be willing to assist.

Teaming Up #4: Rivals and Upstart Companies

Your firm is sure to have rivals who wish to take the competition out of the picture. You may need to do some sniffing them out to find out what they're like and how far they're willing to go. Probably you're best off not straight-out explaining to them your purpose unless you fully trust the people there. But you can set up relationships with people in key positions. Start out by telling them you have an interest in destroying their rival. Give them examples of your espionage and ask if they'd be willing to help you out by making use of your data to thwart the plans of the company you wish to destroy. You might offer your data free-of-charge, or sell it to them. It may *not* be best to go to company higher-ups. You may want to develop relationships with newly-hired college kids looking to make a name for themselves. Look for Yuppie Scum types who have no morals and want to impress their boss, and will use your purloined data to do it.

Teaming Up #5: Similar Motivations

Look at your own motivation and see why you want to destroy the company. For environmental reasons? Then get some radical environmentalists. Be aware they might not see eye-to-eye with you. They may see it more as a case of "let's help the company see the light" rather than "let's put them out of business."

Teaming Up #6: Mercenaries

If you're trying to oust the company as a member of some organization (such as a rival company, a religious group, a cult, a governmental organization, etc.), then you may have funds you can put to use to hire mercenaries to help you out. A mercenary can be anyone who has access to tools, knowledge or physical locations that would be difficult for you to access on your own. Very hard to trust such people since they're just in it for the money and they don't have your good interests at heart. Mercenaries are useful for jobs that are too dirty for you to handle. They can also be used for acts of industrial espionage such as paying the plant-boy to let you take his place for a day. Or striking a deal with an insider, such as with the cleaning crew, security firm, or other hired help that has access to the building.

Teaming Up #7: Community Involvement

Get the community on your side. The Rainforest night club near my house was closed because the township ganged up against them saying they were too noisy. The Transylvania Restaurant in Portland, Oregon, failed (the owners claim) after their disco nights offended the conservative Romanian immigrants who made up the bulk of their patrons, and the local pastor allegedly sermonized harsh words against it.[1] Try to find a rallying point you can use against your target company. Preferably it will be a legitimate gripe, such as noise, but if not you may have to resort to fabrications.

> Another way to locate people to help you is to scour Internet forums, discussion groups, and web sites. You might find bitter brethren who've been scorned by that foul firm. Or you might find people who can provide inside scoops — technical support, customer service reps, customers, or suppliers. Or the president's mom.
>
> You've got to be extremely careful as you take on new partners in crime. You know you can trust yourself, but you can't particularly trust anyone who is unwholesome enough to want to take part in the kind of activities you're inviting them into. "Monkeywrenchers avoid working with people they haven't known for a long time," advises David Foreman, the noted environmental activist, "those who can't keep their mouths closed, and those with grandiose or violent ideas (they may be police agents or dangerous crackpots)."[2] A violent crackpot's power might be harnessed effectively, but a police agent will always be trouble.

Spy organizations have used "plants" and "moles" for years to extract secret information. An agent is planted into foreign territory in order to discover secrets and submit them to his government. Some countries nowadays plant moles into corporations in order to learn about technologies their home companies have not yet developed. They get away with this through various ruses. The Israeli government contracted Recon/Optical, an American company to produce optical technologies for the Israeli military. As part of the bargain, Israel would have two people work on site to monitor progress. Fair enough, right?

Recon/Optical began having doubts a few years into the agreement as they began realizing those two people were soaking up all the information they could regarding the technology under contract, and stuff they had no business sticking their noses into — and doing *something* with it. It was thought they were dispensing the info to another company, Electro-Optics Industries, Ltd., which was able to churn out cheapo knock-off stuff at a much lower price because they didn't have any of that nasty ol' multi-million-dollar R&D investment to recoup. Recon/Optical was a company plummeting fast. They had to dump two-thirds of their workers to survive. Recon/Optical was nearly put out of business by these shenanigans.[3]

Through good times and bad, economies lean and mean, the same old things cause most business failures. In fact, Dun & Bradstreet, which has tracked business failures for many years, finally stopped surveying why businesses fail. D & B's chief economic advisor explains: "We discontinued those surveys because the reasons were very stable. Ninety percent of failures are the result of bad management, and the other big reason is failure to respond to change."[4] Of course many of the attacks throughout here are designed to thrust immediate negative changes at the corporation, with the hope that their response is inadequate. Many companies just don't have the reserve needed to deal with surprises like an unexpected court judgment. The other cause, bad management, is harder to provoke.

That's why some of your most fruitful corporate attacks will come about if you can manage to get some insiders working for you, for your cause, inside the company, or as an independent consultant hired by the company as a manager or accountant. Businesses must spend a bundle on accounting services, yet if the accountant makes mistakes, that can be deadly for the company. Tax forms are lengthy and complicated, and there is much room for error (there's also room for an incompetent accountant to not make use of all the loopholes that a better accountant would know about). One accountant told this story of how he picked up a new client: The client's previous accounting firm signed an agreement with them — then they didn't hear from him for half a year. They thought he was busy filing tax returns, budgeting, establishing internal controls for the business on their behalf. But instead he was doing nothing — and they were paying for it. The company nearly ran out of cash until someone noticed something fishy was going on.[5]

Your team members can also be people who don't have any active involvement with the company, until you introduce them to it. Many companies nowadays routinely practice the obnoxious routine of selling to school children. The group People for the Ethical Treatment of Animals otherwise known as PFTETOA (okay, okay, it's really PETA), enlists the help of the little buggers in their fight against certain corporations. PETA hands out materials such as magazines to be used in the classroom as teaching devices. For instance, a lesson in letter writing based on the horrors of animal testing. After one such lesson, a sixth-grader at the James Martin School in Philadelphia wrote to the chairman of Gillette Co: "Let this be a warning to you. If you hurt another animal, if I find out, one month from [when] this letter arrives to you, I'll bomb your company. P.S. Watch your back."[6] Personally I think this letter, like animal testing, is quite charming. PETA also gives out prizes to kids who spread the word about Gillette's use of animal testing. Now of course I believe wholeheartedly that organizations like Coca Cola and PETA are entirely morally upright and should control our every waking thought (and I also believe we should direct deposit our pay stubs directly into Microsoft's bank accounts). So if companies like these can feed their rhetoric directly to school kids via the mouths of teachers, then certainly no one could object to you doing the same as well. Get all the kids turned off to the company because of animal testing or some other cause kids can relate to, and you'll be raising a new generation of corporate anti-crusaders.

Citations

1. Hofman, Mike. "Disco Nights End on a Downbeat" in *Inc.,* April 1998. p. 29.
2. Foreman, David. *Confessions of an Eco-Warrior.* p. 114.
3. Winkler, Ira. *Corporate Espionage: What it is, Why it is Happening in Your Company, What You Must do About it.* p. 71.
4. Norman, Jan. "Why Firms Fail: It's Not the Economy, Stupid" in *Knight-Ridder/Tribune News Service.* July 29,

1997. p729k3542. States that most businesses fail due to bad management or unexpected change.
5. Daks, Martin. "Hiring Right CPA is Vital: Wrong Advice Can Sink a Start-up Business" in *The Star-Ledger*. June 22, 1998. pp. 57-58.
6. Carton, Barbara. "Teaching Terror?" in *Reader's Digest*. January 1996. p. 148. Originally from *The Wall Street Journal*. Short article telling about PETA's invasion of classrooms to spread its anti-animal-testing messages.

Team Tactics

These tactics make use of teams in one way or another. Some involve teaming up employees against their firm. Other attacks are just too involved to do by yourself. Now that you've got some pals on your side, you can really screw that company good!

Attack #61. Intra-office Sabotage

Hallelujah and praise be the day you start teaming up with employees working inside that depraved corporation you've so long hoped to see fail miserably. When you work for the company you can get away with so much more than you can as a strict outsider. Read any book on scams and cons and you'll come up with dozens of examples of people who bilked the boss, cooked the books, or embezzled funds using their handy dandy inside access to get the run of the place. Consider the case of Jonathan Weis, who stepped out of jail and took on the identity of a recently deceased corporate executive. He used the credentials to obtain an executive position at a company in another part of the country. Once inside the firm he had the clout to instruct the purchasing department to begin purchasing from a new set of suppliers. The new suppliers required payment in advance, but at such steep discounts that it was well worth it. Only Weis knew that this was an elaborate con, the suppliers were run by the Mafia, and after the checks were cashed, both Weis and the suppliers vamoosed fast.[1] Your con doesn't have to be elaborate, any waste will do, and having internal team members on your side will lend the inside edge to your cause of destruction.

Attack #62. Pickets and Protests

A good ol' picketing might do your cause some good. If you're vocal and inventive you can even make the evening news. Come up with a cute visual angle to "sell" your idea to the media, whether that be costumes, effigies, statuaries, or song. If you want them to report on your cause, you have to make your cause interesting. Come up with something good, then send press releases to let them know what's going on. It helps if you picket on a slow news day. And try to get your group as large and diverse and television-ready as possible. Two people with signs is not a T.V. story. A hundred people with signs wearing executioner costumes is the kind of spectacle that the media relishes. The savvy, organized picketer has been known to hire "extras" to beef up the crowd. Another way to increase your exposure is to rally against an already established event. For instance, plan your picket to coincide with the company's annual picnic, or stockholder's meeting, or a press conference to announce an achievement of some sort. Your protest becomes more of an event that way.

True picketers don't use pickets any more — that is, they hold up their cardboard signs in their hands, not attached to picket fence posts. The reason is because they don't want the wooden pickets to be misconstrued as weapons, which is the dumb kind of mistake you'd expect a cop to make. (On the other hand, if you can get employees to picket against their own company you probably do want people arrested since that can only hurt the firm.)

Some businesses respond to protests well. A local fur shop recently found itself the target of weekly protests in front of its store, and they vow to keep coming back until the shop owner agrees to stop selling furs. The owner has no intention of ruining his business just because some people feel like standing outside in the rain every Saturday, and in fact he turned it into a good thing. He acts genially towards them, and has started turning it into a weekly barbecue. Now he's out there with his barbecue grilling, serving up hamburgers and hot dogs to whomever wants it — friends, enemies, customers, protesters. It's his way of making himself look like the good guy, and them the bad guys. To make matters worse for the protesters, at times they've become somewhat rowdy, which also works against them. They've received unfavorable coverage in the newspapers. These are the kinds of situations you want to avoid in your own protests. It's the *company* that should be looking bad, and you all standing there with innocent, puppy-dog sorrow in your eyes.

Prepare your team beforehand so they know exactly what to say to the media. You should have a message planned that makes the company look bad, and does not make you look like a vindictive idiot. Suppose one of you gets on television and starts ranting and raving for ten minutes about the lowlife scum who work for Company X. That only makes you look like a fool. No one will believe you. However, if you speak rationally, articulately, and convey your message in a succinct sound bite or two, then you will get on television and convert others to your cause.

Meanwhile, back at the office... The media is going to be ringing the phones off the hooks trying to get the official side of the story from company hotshots. This is where it can be helpful to have a secretary or receptionist inside the company who does not go out on the picket line. Normally companies are supposed to forward media calls to the media relations person, or publicity department. But your gal on the inside has been prepped to handle media inquiries herself...or to transfer them to someone working with you on this project. Instead of acting calm and rational (which is what the true company spokesperson would do) your shill will become red in the face, blue in the tongue, and scream obscenities at those no-good picketers. The answer to all probing questions should be a suspicious "No comment." If you really get into this, you can have team members call in *pretending* to be journalists trying to get the company's side of the story. Patch those calls directly to the real P.R. department. That way they'll be barking up the wrong tree and won't suspect a thing.[2]

Attack #63. False Trends

Start a false trend by having team members mail suggestions and complaints to the company president. Suppose the president of a clothing company starts receiving correspondence from unrelated people all over the country, who praise his jeans but just wish they came in orange and green, and were a little bit smaller, because his current sizes are too baggy. The company president might start taking these requests seriously, figuring he's hot on some new trend, and he'll start testing the waters with orange and green jeans (ugly), which are several sizes smaller than usual (too small for most people who are overweight anyway). Since the whole thing was a false trend, nobody's interested and he just wasted valuable resources pursuing a wild goose chase that you led him on. For best results, have several of your team members from all over the country write in using different mediums (mail, e-mail, fax) and pretending to be teenagers reporting on the hot new trend at their high school.

You can release to the company industry reports or surveys showing which kinds of customers are more eager to buy, spend more money on certain kinds of products, or will retain services longer. Sprinkle authoritative sources throughout, and let the long-term planners get hold of this (falsified) data, and they'll plan themselves into a financial quandary.

Your inside team can stuff corporate suggestion boxes with ideas that will cause grumbling. "I wish we'd go back to a full day's work on summer Fridays. Lots of us don't like having to come in for just a half day and then go home." Anything to drive down morale! (Be sure to use phony handwriting or type it up so as to be anonymous.)

Public relations firms have grown savvier and savvier at coming up with ways to fake out companies — and the general public at large. One method is to set up a hotline for people to call in for more information on an issue. When they call they speak to a telemarketer, who feeds the caller a number of facts and sound bites, clarifying the issue for them. The telemarketer whips up the caller into a rabid frenzy, then asks how would they like to tell their congressperson directly? They say, "Of course!," never suspecting the next move — the telemarketer patches the call directly through to the congressperson's office. To the congressperson and staff it seems as though they're receiving a rash of unrelated calls from individual concerned citizens.[3] This tactic can be changed to patch in calls to a company president, CEO, or influential people with whom the company does business. A similar tactic has been used to create mass handwritten letters. They whip up the caller into a frenzy, ask if they'd like to write a letter to so-and-so to speak their mind — most callers will calm down and not do it, but the telemarketing staff writes up the letter for them, using appropriate stationery (strong, bold, corporate paper for a senior executive; cute kitty cat stationery for a little-ol'-grandma-type), and sends it in to create the illusion of a massive outpouring of epistolary concern by American citizens. And really now, however in the world can the company president resist the charms of cute kitty-cat stationery?

Attack #64. Strikes

When workers strike they're usually thinking about getting what they want, not striking themselves out of jobs. But strikes are harmful to companies in many ways, so it would be useful to your cause if a strike could be arranged.

Start by creating a pissed-off workforce by driving them insane with all sorts of annoyances as we've been discussing. You might be able to find some rallying point that the workforce can get behind and support. That's what workers did at Leslie's Poolmart Inc. in North Hollywood, California.[4] When Philip Leslie was ousted from his own company by a leveraged buyout, hundreds of employees stayed home or picketed their own stores. The company was effectively shut down while this went on. Leslie was able to swing this support because the workers saw him as loyal to them, and they were outraged by the way he was being treated. (And it didn't hurt that he promised them jobs at his new company if they got fired from this one.)

If there haven't been any popular-guy firings lately, and no other opportunity presents itself, you may be able to instigate some mishap to occur, then slyly shift blame to management, and use it as an excuse to strike. You can borrow Leslie's idea and encourage workers by promising them jobs at your own rival company. You must possess strong leadership skills, or team up with insiders in the company who do. Convince the workers they can do better than what they're being paid now, and tell 'em you have other jobs waiting for them in the wings if this doesn't work out. Then strike!

There are different kinds of strikes. There is the no-more-work-till-our-demands-are-met strike. There are sit-ins (in which workers do show up for work, but then they refuse to move); and the sick-out (in which a mysterious malady seems to be infecting everyone at the plant, and who can argue with illness as long as you have a nicely forged doctor's note?). There's the "slowdown strike" in which workers show up for work, but they do half the job they're capable of, and make many costly mistakes in the process. This is a good one because it's hard for the bosses to chastise employees who are showing up for work and seem to be trying to do a good job — especially when it's everyone in the company doing a lousy job. A variation is when workers follow all the bureaucratic rules that have been set up, even to the point of absurdity. It's like a piece of satirical performance art as the workers all suddenly become the most dedicated rule-followers in the world, and become extremely concerned with following every rule to the letter. The result is chaos and a backlog of undone work. Then there's the "selective strike" which involves randomly striking or not showing up for work over a period of time. For two days everyone's out, then everyone shows up again a day, and the next day they're out again. This unpredictability prevents the bosses from hiring scabs, and hopefully forces the bosses, who don't know how to do any real work, into the positions of the striking workers. With all the on-again-off-again behavior, the bosses, and any scabs they do manage to hire, end up pretty dazed and confused at what's going on.

The key to all these tactics is *solidarity.* As explained in *How To Fire Your Boss — A Worker's Guide To Direct Action* an excellent on-line manual of workplace subversion:

> If one worker stands up and protests, the bosses will squash him or her like a bug. Squashed bugs are obviously of little use to their families, friends, and social movements in general. But if all the workers stand up together, the boss will have no choice but to take you seriously. S/he can fire any individual worker who makes a fuss, but s/he might find it difficult to fire their entire workforce.

It is said that strikes hurt more nowadays than they did fifteen or twenty years ago, because companies run leaner now. Firms are geared towards just-in-time delivery, which means they don't carry large stockpiles of inventory. If a strike hits, there's not much product lying around to sell. The figure oft-cited lately is the one from General Motor's March 1996 strike. Three thousand employees from their Dayton, Ohio, plant struck, the company closed 59 assembly and parts plants, which left 81,000 GM workers sitting idle on their bums. (Another source claims 177,000 workers,[5] who knows?) The end result was GM showed a $387 million loss for first quarter 1996, as compared with $1.6 million profit the same period one year earlier.[6] A strike by some workers can have major consequences all throughout a company — and in the companies which that company does business with, for many of GM's part suppliers themselves had to lay off thousands of workers because they relied so much on GM's business.[7]

Try to conduct your strike during a busy time of year. David Wyss, research director at DRI/McGraw-Hill, an economic consulting company, said, "August is a good time for a strike, because there is not a lot of stuff being done."[8] Well what's a "good time for a strike" for the company is *not* a good time for a strike for *you* because what you want is bad for the company. Wyss was referring specifically to a United Parcel Service strike in 1997. The summer months tend to be slow, so you *don't* want to start your strike then. Autumn tends to be busier for many businesses, so is a better choice to pick.

One potential problem of strikes are scabs and strike breakers. In some cases workers have fought back in various ways. Before striking, workers can hide or remove necessary pieces of equipment from the factory, so that scabs won't be able to operate the machinery. Or they may team up to ensure that the scabs hired are among their own group. Regina Barreca in her book on revenge asks, "When you hear the old union organizer's tale about the company that hired a hundred out-of-town scabs to replace striking factory workers, and paid the scabs' train fares to the site, only to have them disappear once they arrived (they were themselves union members from this distant town), do you feel like cheering?"[9] Rah, rah, rah!

If a company does business with many other companies, the strike can have a ripple-down effect. During that aforementioned U.P.S. strike, other companies couldn't ship out their products as effectively with their regular shipper on strike. Some companies had piles of stock accumulating in warehouses. Others had to switch to higher-priced shippers, reducing profit margins. Others had to start laying off workers. Companies were unable to deliver products on schedules they had promised. All sorts of side problems emerged from the strike of one corporation. "If the strike continues, it's going to shut us down," said the V.P. of a cowboy-hat company.[10] This brings up the idea of another way to use strikes to your benefit: Attack them when they're down. Under circumstances such as these, the company's like a fist wrapped firmly around a hand grenade about to explode. This is the perfect opportunity to start coming at them with some of the other attacks in these pages. Their grip will loosen. The company explodes.

⌨ **www.au.iww.org/labor/direct_action/title.html** How to Fire Your Boss — a Worker's Guide to Direct Action. This web site is run by BossBusters, a project of the Bay Area Wobblies. They wish to "counteract the day to day drudgery of contemporary wageslavery..." by "guerrilla warfare that cripples the boss' ability to make a profit and makes him/her cave in to the workers' demands."

Attack #65. Legal Action

See if you can sue your target company for anything, anything at all. Being sued just might be the most costly thing in the world. Consider the poor case of Lyle Stuart, publisher of controversial books, who was sued by Steve Wynn over an unflattering mention of the casino tycoon in a book catalog.[11] Wynn won. Stuart found himself hit in the head with a $3 million dollar verdict slapped against him. (And Stuart's entire inventory of books was frozen, which meant he couldn't even sell books to make money to pay the verdict. Or legal fees for that matter.) This sort of debt makes staying in business not easy, and Stuart unfortunately did not hold libel insurance, as many publishers do. "He's not the first person to lose a lawsuit and go out of business," commented a lawyer specializing in First Amendment issues of this kind. The editor of one tabloid newspaper, speaking on a cable television show[12] said that one libel suit could eat up profits for the next *five* years. Yikes!

At one company I found an urgent memo circulating that a new product could not be shipped because the company had discovered, to its chagrin, that it did not hold the legal ownership of the copyright as it thought it did. Most likely the product would have to be canceled after months of work getting it together for sale, putting it into the catalog, selling it to various retail stores around the country, and placing additional orders for manufacture. What a waste of time and money if all that were to come to naught. Perhaps as you do your own shuffling through the files, you'll come across a confidential memo detailing some legal entanglement the company knows about but is ignoring (and wouldn't the competition like to know about that). Or perhaps it's an illegality that people across the United States would be outraged about if they heard it on the nightly news. Everything is actionable nowadays, and if you can convince people to be angry over something, no doubt the company will be sued. If nothing legit comes out, the very least you can do is make up a fake scare, sending a threat letter to them.

A company being sued will be offered advice by its legal counsel, which if you're doing your investigative homework, you should have in the palm of your hand. Any advice that they give becomes a means of attack. For instance, often lawyers will advise not to throw away or shred documents pertaining to the case. This may be the only time in your life you volunteer to take out the trash. Rip up and discard documents containing relevant data, then clue in the opposing legal team of your "findings." Boy will they be pleased.

Below is a letter found in some doctors' medical practice. This could be used to attack the doctors, if that was the goal, showing how the medical practice was knowingly giving less-than-optimal care. If you were attacking the hospital, you might find these letters in their files and you would thus want to contact the doctors for their information to help you bring down the hospital. It's also an example of what we discussed earlier — how the best information might not come from the company itself (the hospital) but from smaller businesses that do business with the company (in this case a medical practice).

Dr. Albert Tongue
13 Sunningdale Drive
Thomas Jefferson Hospital
Stomach Ache, PA 01010

Dear Dr. Tongue:

I have become increasingly concerned (as have many of our colleagues) with the recording of obviously inaccurate calorie counts on charts at TJ Hospital with the subsequent completely invalid, misleading and worthless nutritional assessments that are derived from these counts. Two examples are enclosed with the patients' ID obscured. On 4/13 the Nutrition note states that the patient had a calorie count of 535. However, lunch, snacks and non-hospital food brought in to the patient is not included. This is a worthless exercise. It would be better to record "no accurate count available" than to record a knowingly inaccurate number. Should a reviewer hastily look at the chart they will assume we are malnourishing our patients. These efforts have been expensive, valueless wastes of time that make our charts look bad.

The next issue involves the inferior monitoring equipment present in the bronchoscopy suite. The EKG readout is not very visible and much too short, and the respirations are always wrong because they have EKG artifact in the readout, giving a typical respiratory rate of 50-70 breaths a minute. Perhaps a second nurse should be on duty because of the poor quality of the monitoring equipment.

The final, and perhaps most important and clearly the most disturbing issue is that we do not have any nurses and/or technicians at this time cross-trained to perform bronchoscopy. This is inexcusable. I have had several patients at our hospital who may have not received optimal care because bronchoscopy was not available. This should not and can not continue, and the director of bronchoscopy must make this issue a priority (and actually do something about it for a change!).

In closing, I hope this letter will be taken seriously and the above matters resolved in an expedient and appropriate manner, resulting in an improvement in our hospital.

Sincerely,
Dr. Santa Cruz

So find some rhyme or reason, and then sue. Well, not you sue personally, you don't have that kind of money. But maybe you can get a Class A suit going with fellow shlubs who've been scorned by that heartless company, or perhaps you can find an irate ex-employee who feels they were fired unjustly and will sue on basis of racial or sexual discrimination. Maybe if you've got a strong enough case you might be able to drum up tears and support from some liberal group, or even reduced fees from some head-in-the-clouds lawyer.

One final way to use legal action against the company is if they're being sued, or even if they are being threatened with being sued, some customers or stockholders might get worried and start having doubts about the company. In a confidential memo at one company I found a boss ordering his underlings: "Continue selling [a particular product] as planned. Please assure your customers that the recent court action has no impact on [that product]." It then switched tones, saying, "THIS INFORMATION IS FOR DISCUSSION ONLY. IT IS NOT FOR SHARING IN WRITTEN FORM TO CUSTOMERS." And what the customer doesn't know, may not hurt them, but it sure might hurt the company...

Attack #66. Internal Rumors

Rumors can go around inside a company as well as outside. Inside rumors work on the mental-anguish principle. They cause employees to work poorly or not at all, or they redirect workers' attentions away from where they should be focused. Internal conflict is one of the key factors often associated with business failures. "Rumor mills cost money, lots of money," warns Jack Stack, president and CEO of the Springfield Re-manufacturing Corporation. "They are the most expensive form of corporate communication around. They breed fear, mistrust, divisiveness, unrealistic expectations, and ignorance. They take all the problems a company has and make them worse. For that, you pay through the nose."[13] Stack's solution is to host regular staff meetings to keep employees abreast of goings-ons. My solution is to do everything possible to keep the rumor mill grinding away.

Start by finding someone who works for the company and cultivate him to be on your side as discussed earlier. Then help him start planting rumors such as these.

If they do urine tests of employees, see about planting drugs on some bigshot. Make sure word gets around the whole company, and is leaked to the media as well.

Larger companies may have an office where employee grievances are registered. Find its files and you'll have a treasure trove of complaints levied by one employee against another. Use this inside knowledge to plan nasty rumors, pitting co-workers against one another.

Start a rumor that the head honchos from corporate headquarters are coming to visit. Local managers will go crazy preparing the building, mowing the lawn, washing the walls, pruning hedges, agitating nervously, and sweating needlessly all for a boss who never shows.

Less drastic rumors may also be effective, like if the bosses think there's a general discontent in the workforce. Your insider crony can drop hints or suggestions in the suggestion box that beneath exterior smiles there lie disgruntled malcontents. Shareholders might attend the annual meeting and raise seemingly pressing issues during the question and answer sessions. Managers tend to overreact to problems, often instituting changes quickly, without thought. If employees weren't mad before, they'll start getting mad now! As Jack Stack says: "Let's say you have a hundred people, and one guy is constantly complaining. It's easy to start thinking morale is bad because of that one guy. He gets you down, and he may lead you to institute policies or make changes that put the other ninety-nine at risk."[14]

■▟■▟■▟■▟■▟■▟■

Attack #67. Turn Their Customers Against Them

Do whatever you can to turn the company's customers against them. The business books tell us it takes seven times the cost and effort to win back a dissatisfied customer as it did to acquire them in the first place (and it costs an incredible amount to win new customers in the first place). Big customers are the obvious customers to turn, but smaller customers may cause headaches as well. You may find certain customers concerned more with quality than price, and certainly those are prime candidates too since they're apparently willing to spend anything. Start messing with the quality and they'll be searching for a new supplier to do business with.

Let me tell you a tale about one company whose customers turned against them, and the resulting squalls it caused. A very large publishing company purchased a small chain of bookstores and had the great idea of selling its backlist and remainder (cheaper) titles in those stores. It was a way of attaching their product to a somewhat known chain of stores. But some small clients (i.e., small bookstores) got wind of the plan, and they thought the publisher's book stores would be competing with them. It would be monopolistic, and the parent company was already being sued for unlawfully using its size against smaller competitors. One of the small store owners threatened to call *Publisher's Weekly* and raise holy Hell. The megalith backed down and abandoned the project. Now keep in mind that before backing down, they had already invested money in the project:

- They had scouted locations for stores.

- They had leases on storefronts in strip malls.

- They had purchased fixtures and shelves for use in stores.

- Not to mention time and money invested in negotiations, legal counsel, time lost from other projects while in planning meetings, and all the work done on this project that ultimately went spiraling around to nowhere.

This was a big $70 million company and it backed down at the slightest provocation, because a few customers turned against them. The stores went out of business even before they were in business to begin with!

Attack #68. Cold Call for the Company

Cold call for the company. Identify yourself as a representative of the company and offer fabulous deals that will be impossible to deliver. Or offer deals that are much worse than the competition. Be a pesky salesperson. Call back again and again. Cold calling can be a lot of work as any salesperson knows, so divvy up the customer list amongst your team members. Have each team member do a little bit of cold calling. Especially cold call to influential people and potential customers who will be really pissed and decide not to buy from such a reprehensible company. When a customer service company surveyed businesses, nearly 50% responded that they would never do business with a company after being treated rudely by them on the telephone. Respondents listed rude behavior like leaving them on hold, transferring calls to the wrong department, failing to answer the phone promptly, answering in an un-businesslike manner ("Yeah, and what do you want?"), and screening calls like little busybodies.[15] I'm sure if you put your mind to it you can do all these and a lot worse. Keep it rude, keep it crude, but keep it believable too. You want the customer put off, but not so put off he'll suspect it's a prank. A side benefit of this attack is you can use it to learn exactly what the customers like and dislike about the company's products and services, which can be exposed (if damaging) or attacked (if beneficial to the company) accordingly. If you find yourself in tune with what the customer is looking for, or objects to, in certain products, that too can be useful. With the knowledge that the customer is looking for X and despises Y, you can slyly let it slip to the company's (real) sales rep that the company absolutely adores Y while loathing X. The sales reps will henceforth handle sales calls entirely backwards — selling suspenders when the client wants a belt. And what if with all your bungling you still manage to make a sale for the company? Why, give it to the competition of course.

Attack #69. Too Much of a Good Thing

One attack that everyone loves perpetrating is a "good work strike." The idea is that employees start performing their jobs so efficiently that they end up hurting the company. The company has trouble detecting malfeasance since everyone is supposedly doing a good job. Caretakers at Mercy Hospital in France wanted to strike against their boss, but didn't want patients to suffer. Instead they did just the opposite: lavished all their attention on providing excellent service to patients. Meanwhile they were letting billing slips and paperwork pile up; essentially they were providing care for free. In three days the hospital's income was cut in half. (The administrators gave in to workers' demands at that point, which of course was the workers' goal. You'd have a different goal.) Similar actions have been taken by transportation workers (who would forget to collect fares); and restaurant workers, who doubled the food, and rounded down the checks.

Of course this sort of thing goes on accidentally as well. Companies routinely go out of business because employees don't know how to manage the work-to-money ratio of business. Business owner and writer Jack Stack points out that commissioned salespeople often ruin a company. They think "the more sales, the better:"

The trouble is, more sales may not be good for the company. Commissioned salespeople can cause chaos. While they're out selling everything they can, the producers can't keep up. So what happens? Eventually the company goes out of business, leaving everyone out of work. Or it fires the experienced salespeople and replaces them with younger, cheaper talent. It has to do something, because the salespeople are making too much money, and the company isn't profitable.[16]

Attack #70. Start a Disinformation Campaign

Corporate executives are naturally competitive, and very, very stupid. If one were able to delve inside their mushy little brains, one would find an overactive Gimmie Gland, pumping Want Hormones throughout their sweaty bodies. Want is the hormone that induces executives to always need to purchase the most expensive television sets, automobiles, automatic bread makers, barbecue grills, and penile implants. These quasi-humans especially exhibit these behaviors on the corporate battlefield. For instance, if they see that a competing company *has something* or *does something* that they have-not, or do-not, they must suddenly *have that thing* or *do that thing* too.

Even if it makes no sense to have it or do it, off they go on a wild go-get-it go-do-it spree:

Executive #1: "The CEO of Rival Corporation said in *Forbes* they're introducing a new bran cereal to produce livelier bowel movements."

Executive #2: "We should also manufacture bran cereals. I'll have my team reconfigure the automotive assembly line to produce bran cereal."

Executive #3: "We can go one step better, and actually offer the bowel movements as a special bonus right inside the box."

See what I mean?

This technique of disinformation was used to great effect by the Reagan administration. They all yakked up the Star Wars defense program so much, the Soviets started believing such a fantasy was actually possible. Feeling it had to respond, the Soviet Union nearly spent itself into bankruptcy trying to account for the Star Wars program. As you know, the program never materialized to any significant degree. How many companies have done the same to their competitors?[17]

You can approach the company as representing a consulting group, investigative firm, or industry analysis. Offer to sell them competitive information, insider information that they have no right to know, or if they're not game for that, say you have statistics and breakdowns of the marketplace that they can't get from any other source. They take the bait. You waste their time, their money perhaps, and misdirect them from true goals with the false data you present to them.

Simple threats might do the trick. When Philip Leslie stood by helplessly, watching his own company being sold off to the highest bidder, he swore to each prospective buyer "that if they bought the company, I'd go into business against them and pulverize them." His former business partners, who were selling off the company, complained that his threats cost them millions of dollars in the sale.[18]

Guy Kawasaki, the president of a small software company, was looking through his company database and noticed the name of a rival in it.[19] The rival was product manager of competing software at a much larger company. As a way to mess with his mind, Kawasaki sent the guy a company coffee mug with a letter explaining that the company was so successful they were sending this gift to all customers, thanking them for their support. While the larger firm "didn't go out and spend thousands of dollars on mugs for its customers" it accomplished something or other. It gave him a laugh anyway, and maybe if you try this trick you will cause the company to bankrupt itself into delivering primo customer service. Who knows?

Attack #71. Increase Their Confidence

Most new products fail — because the world really doesn't need any new cereals with purple marshmallows or peanut butter shampoo, or whatever the latest launch is. So if a product is going to fail, might as well help the company to make it a *big failure*. One way is to find out about product tests and skew them in favor of the product (the more horrible the product, the better).

Read the trade journals, do all the research you can (and continue the internal snooping we talked about earlier), and you'll find out when and where and why and how new products are being test marketed by that company, and you'll figure out a way to skew the results. Marketing consultant Robert McMath writes in his book *What Were They Thinking?* about how when a new shampoo called Wash & Comb was being test marketed all the competing shampoo-makers bought up thousands of the bottles so they could study it and see if it posed a threat to their business. His company alone bought 3,000 bottles. The company who made Wash & Comb were amazed at the great sales figures, and so went ahead and rolled out the product nationally. It bombed. McMath says he always tries to contact companies when his consulting firm buys products, so they can keep their numbers in perspective, but of course executives at major companies don't like to hear bad news. They want to believe that 3,000 bottles of shampoo were bought by gullible American housewives, not by competitors and consultants trying to reverse engineer the product. In another case, McMath's firm was hired by Hunt Wesson, the company that owns Orville Reddenbacher popcorn, to buy up samples of a new competing popcorn being test marketed. "First, we cleaned out the store shelves. Then we went directly to the Grand Union warehouse to purchase by the case. Time after time. All told, we sent hundreds of cases to Hunt Wesson. A Grand Union executive told us that we were just about the only people buying the product."[20] McMath knew he had destroyed the test, and he goody-two-shoedly called executives at the rival popcorn firm to let them know their popcorn was being bought by his consulting group, and not avid popcorn fans. The messages went unanswered, the dismal-selling product was rolled out nationally, and it too was a product that popped, fizzled, whatever you want to call it.

Okay, one more example (my favorite). Towards the end of the 1960s, Wilson Harrel was selling his cleaning solution Formula 409 and had gathered a fairly sizable chunk of the market share for cleaning products. Then Harrel learned Proctor & Gamble was test marketing a rival cleaner called Cinch in Denver, Colorado. Harrel took the unintuitive step of discouraging stores from restocking Formula 409, and he ceased advertising and promotions in Denver. Cinch sales soared far beyond what P & G could have predicted, and they rubbed their greedy hands together and rolled out Cinch nationwide. So far it's the same old story. But here's the rest of the story:

Now that Harrel had them thinking great expectations, he knocked them out with his next move. Harrel bundled together the sixteen-ounce Formula 409 with the half-gallon size, and sold the two together for $1.48 (very cheap price, especially for the two products together). He figured anyone who bought a half gallon plus sixteen ounces of the stuff wouldn't need to buy any more cleaning products for six months. Harrel plugged in the advertising machine and promoted the hell out of this deal. Everyone who normally used Formula 409, and many people who didn't, made sure to take advantage of this great deal. Everyone else — well, there hardly was anyone else left over to buy Cinch, and less than a year later, Cinch was ditched.[21]

The moral is this: Corporations are so stupid they think that just because they release a new brand of shampoo, cleaning product, or popcorn, that people are really going to run to the store and purchase massive quantities of it, brag to their friends about what a great new product is out there, and keep going back to buy more and more of the stuff. Corporations are so stupid they really believe this!

So if these consulting groups and rivals can trick companies into acting this way, so can you. If you hear word of a product being test marketed by a company, try to see that it gets bought up (preferably by your team using double-coupons and other money-saving devices so the company won't be making any profit on it). Or donate the products to a local homeless shelter. Just make sure it gets bought up and out of the hands of real consumers.

Entrepreneurs of all stripes start up businesses in the first place because they're so gosh darned gung ho. The trouble is, that same passion that fires them up, can burn them to char if they're not careful — or if you fuel their fire. If your target company is a small business, especially a new venture, you can increase their confidence in several ways. The proprietor of one sports memorabilia company, fueled by his own gung ho overdrive, went almost three years without salary, wasting well over $100,000 of his own money, and siphoning off his children's college funds — before finally going out of business.

"I could have played golf and watched TV for the last five years, and I'd have more money than I do now," said this entrepreneur in a pitiful statement. "The blinders-on, full-speed-ahead mentality sounds great, and it really does motivate people. But the sad truth is that 'never give up' isn't always the right thing. For people like me, it means we burn through our savings."[22] The problem was, he sold a good product. People loved what he sold, and the products elicited loving comments from notables like Wayne Gretzky, Bruce Jenner, and Babe Ruth's granddaughter. These testimonials warmed his heart and kept him going... and going right down the toilet for far too long. *They clouded his vision.* They took his eyes and mind off more important things: like the numbers.

You can do the same thing, provide testimonials (real or fake) to boost their ego. On the same day that these gee-whiz-golly letters come in, call up the place and inquire about placing an order for a thousand — no *two* thousand — of their items. Don't make a deal, but put it in their head that people like what they sell, and they're itching to buy. Ideally you can induce them to extend themselves too far over the edge, exceed their capital, use up their resources, produce too much product, and get backlogged in mountains of inventory.

Attack #72. Pry Open Partnerships

Find other businesses and organizations that do business with your company, and attack them. Why go to other places? One reason is they may be easier. "To bypass the protection mechanisms... intelligence agencies frequently compromise third- or fourth-party organizations, who have weak or no security, to obtain access to their primary target. While the third parties may not suffer a direct loss, they will eventually be affected, perhaps by paying more for the services received or by losing a customer."[23] Winkler points out that all people, businesses, and organizations interact with a wide network of other people, businesses, and organizations. A mom-and-pop pizza shop in Washington, D.C., may be the first to know when a governmental crisis is brewing, since they start getting late-night calls from the Pentagon.[24]

Almost everyone does certain basic things like buy food, fill up a tank of gas, go to the dry cleaners, or stop at the deli for a sandwich. All these small local businesses become potentially useful in one way or another. Many of the attacks throughout this book are applicable at other locations besides the business itself, and in fact it may be easier and less suspicious to perform those attacks someplace else, which is why you should keep these other places in mind for attacks like vehicle assaults, espionage, team-building, and rumors.

Citations

1. Whitlock, Chuck. *Chuck Whitlock's Scam School.* pp. 140-141.
2. Lynn, Jacquelyn. "Fighting Back: What to do When Picketers Pick on You" in *Entrepreneur.* February 1996. p. 84. Management's side to the picket story, how they deal with picketing, offering some ideas on how to keep them from handling the picket appropriately. This article was useful for generating ideas for this section.
3. Stauber, John and Sheldon Rampton. *Toxic Sludge is Good for You!, Lies, Damn Lies and the Public Relations Industry.* p. 97.
4. Emshwiller, John R. "Desire for Revenge Fuels an Entrepreneurr's Ambition: How a Successful Partnership Went Sour and Turned Into an All-Out War" in *The Wall Street Journal,* April 19, 1991. p. B2.
5. Brittan, David. "When Bad Things Happen to Good Factories" in *Technology Review.* July 1996. p. 14. Article on the GM strike, just-in-time systems, and setting up factory systems that will flow effectively.
6. Lucas, Allison. "Damage Control" in *Sales & Marketing Management.* June 1996. p. 21. Article on the effects of strikes on just-in-time inventory system companies.
7. Brittan, p. 14.
8. Johnson, Dirk. "Small Businesses Suffer the Most From U.P.S. Strike / Unshipped Goods Pile Up / Corporations Weather Storm, but Worry About Effects of a Longer Walkout" in *The New York Times.* August 9, 1997. p. 9.
9. Barreca, Regina. *Sweet Revenge: The Wicked Delights of Getting Even.* p. 107.

10. Johnson, Dirk. p. 9.
11. Carvajal, Doreen. "Defamation Suit Leaves Small Publisher Near Extinction" in *The New York Times.* October 8, 1997. p. D1. About Lyle Stuart's Barricade Books sued by Steve Wynn because his feelings were hurt over a reference in a catalog description.
12. *Tabloid Frenzy* on The Learning Channel.
13. Stack, Jack. *The Great Game of Business.* Currency, Doubleday. New York. 1992. p. 180. Stack details his strategy for corporate success. Basically it is, be honest with employees, tell them the numbers your company needs to achieve to be profitable, and that will motivate them to succeed.
14. *Ibid.*, p. 46.
15. Marchetti, Michelle. "Dial 'R' for Rudeness" in *Sales & Marketing Management.* December 1995. p. 33. Short article based on a survey by a customer service group explaining the importance of being nice on the phone, and the consequences of not doing so.
16. Stack, p. 69.
17. Winkler, Ira. *Corporate Espionage: What it is, Why it is Happening in Your Company, What You Must do About it,* p. 23.
18. Emshwiller, p. B2.
19. Kawasaki, George. *How to Drive Your Competition Crazy: Creating Disruption for Fun and Profit.* p. 191.
20. McMath, Robert M and Thom Forbes. *What Were They Thinking? Marketing Lessons I've Learned From Over 80,000 New-Product Innovations and Idiocies.* Times Business, Random House, New York. 1998. p. 86. The author pulls out items from his museum of failed products,

and explains why they failed, how they could have been improved, or why the companies shouldn't have bothered in the first place.

21. Kawasaki, pp. 192-193.
22. Useem, Jerry. "Failure: The secret of my success" in *Inc.* May 1998. p. 67. Article about businesses that fail due to overconfidence of the entrepreneur running it.
23. Winkler, Ira. pp. 57-58.
24. *Ibid.*, p. 58.

Meetings

If you've ever held a job in corporate America, you might have noticed the similarity between meetings and rodeos — a lot of bullshit flying around. Now that you're anti-corporate America, there are two kinds of meetings you need to be concerned with: productive meetings and unproductive meetings. It is your job to extend and create unproductive meetings, while disrupting and destroying any productive meeting.

For instance, let's say the company is having a very significant problem — someone is continuously smearing feces on the ceiling tiles. (Hmmm, I wonder who?) So the company president calls a meeting to get to the bottom of this mystery. Now this is what I would call an unproductive or bad meeting. It's a stupid meeting! It takes people away from their work, but it doesn't help the company's bottom line in any way. You want this sort of meeting to last as long as possible. If you can extend the meeting (by asserting dissenting opinions, or having the employees rally against the horrendous working conditions), then you will be effectively wasting company time and money. If it's a smaller company, all the employees might be engaged in the meeting simultaneously, so they might end up missing crucial sales calls or if it's a technical company, there could be frustrated customers calling in, trying to get technical support. So it is in your best interest to facilitate stupid meetings like this.

On the other hand there are productive meetings which, if allowed to continue, might actually accomplish something. For example, if the top salesperson is meeting with a client who wants to buy millions of dollars worth of product, that could turn out to be a very productive meeting, so you should do everything in your power to disrupt it, anger the millionaire client, and make the salesperson look like a fool.

One last thing. Some meetings rely on teleconferencing, telephone technology that allows many participants from all over the country to join together in one phone call that is broadcast from a speaker system to the meeting room. If a company uses this form of meeting, you are likely to discover memos beforehand giving the time, date, dial-in number, and possibly code numbers used to dial in to the teleconference. Your espionage will pay off handsomely if you can listen in to a meeting like that just by dialing in on the telephone.

In this section we will look at some ways to induce useless, unproductive meetings, and we will also look at ways to break up the important ones.

Attack #73. Mess Up Their Meeting Rooms

If you know there's a meeting tomorrow, mess up their meeting rooms tonight. After they spent countless hours overtime making sure everything was prepared for the big meeting, won't they be dripping with sweat when they walk in, in the morning, and see what you've done to the place — and they only have fifteen minutes to clean it up!

- Damage window blinds so they can't be shut properly. Sunlight streaming in will lighten up their slide presentation or hit 'em in the eye.

- Scratch obscenities in their big ol' mahogany conference table.

- Remove batteries from remote control for slide projector or TV/VCR console. Or clear and reprogram the control then lose the battery.

- Use permanent markers on whiteboards that are meant to be used with erasable markers only. Steal the erasers while you're at it.

- Perhaps you can place bugs, or a tape recorder, or somehow listen in to the meeting to gain confidential information.

- Pour maple syrup on all the chairs.

Get in there, look around at the place, and you'll be inspired to come up with a whole lot more you can do.

Attack #74. Food

Food can be used as a way of busting into a meeting, gaining entry to overhear, plant listening devices, or who knows what. Don Peppers, a well known ad exec once desperately needed to find a miracle way to break into a meeting as a way of promoting his own business. He and his partner ordered some pizzas and waited outside the meeting room for when the hotel staff would be entering with their own cart of food. At the tone of one o'clock, Peppers and partner barged right in behind the hotel staff. They strutted their stuff, delivered the pizzas — and a short presentation and the materials they'd prepared telling the executives about their agency — then they beat it out of there.[1] You can follow their lead, using food as a method of entry, to overhear, overspy, assert an opposing viewpoint, or plant some sort of disruptive influence in the room.

Meetings are notorious feasts, filled with food and drink of all kinds. If you can get at the food, you can possibly bring down a whole bunch of executives all at once, and wouldn't that be a pity. Below is the last page of a three-page memo from a mid-sized company, outlining how one of their sales meetings is to be set up. Your espionage should come up with similar documents about your own target company.

When you find notes like these you'll have an idea of what food will be served, and perhaps who will be doing the catering. It helps you prepare beforehand. Knowing that cookies will be served lets you bake up your own batch of cookies with Ex-Lax or marijuana baked into it. You also have the chance to introduce some food poisoning or LSD into the eats. Or slip some sleeping drugs into the food or drink. Shake up their soda cans. Whatever it takes to damage or embarrass the firm, or make the meeting ineffective.

SPECS FOR UPCOMING SALES FORCE MEETING

Clarke Ballrooms 1 & 2 — Meeting from 9-12 and from 1:30-4:30

ROOM SET UP — Room needs to be set up by 7:30 a.m.

Schoolroom for 70 people with a headtable for 10 people
Four 6-foot tables in the back of the room to display materials on

AUDIO VISUAL
5 microphones at the head table

FOOD AND BEVERAGE
8:30 a.m. — 60 people
Continental breakfast for 50 people

10:30 am
Whatever juice and food is left from the continental breakfast. Freshly brewed coffee, decaffeinated coffee and assorted teas for 50 people. Individual bottled juices on an as consumed basis

LUNCH BUFFET IN THE ATRIUM LOUNGE AT 12:00
Italian buffet for 55 people
Freshly brewed coffee, decaffeinated coffee and assorted teas
assorted soft drinks on an as consumed basis

3:00 p.m. FOOD AND BEVERAGE IN CLARKE BALLROOM 1 & 2
Freshly Brewed coffee, decaffeinated coffee and assorted teas for 50 people
Bottled mineral water on an as consumed basis
Assorted soft drinks on an as consumed basis
4 dozen assorted giant cookies
2 dozen fruit yogurts, assorted (include some nonfat yogurts)
1 dozen granola bars

Attack #75. Gum Up the Workers

"Are you going to the meeting?" asked the administrative assistant.

"What meeting?"

"Didn't you get that memo? See it there — "

TO: DEPARTMENT MANAGERS AND STAFF

RE: REORGANIZATION MEETING — PLEASE DISTRIBUTE

The reorganization meeting scheduled for today has been postponed until 3:00 p.m. Anyone interested in finding out how these changes will affect you and your department are urged to attend. Conference room A2. Refreshments will be served.

The words were chilling. Slightly vague, somewhat ominous. Photocopied onto crisp white papers tossed casually into in-boxes up and down the floor. No one knew exactly what it meant, and the room was crowded with curious staff at 3:00 p.m. They wondered and waited, and talked amongst themselves, and ate the refreshments, and sat around wasting time. Some of them picked up the information kits that were distributed around the meeting room.

No one knew that *you* had called this meeting, secretly, to waste time, to provide a distraction while rummaging through desks, to plant sinister seeds of mistrust and confusion, to keep them from more important work. Good work!

The opposite attack works well too — locate meeting memos in in-baskets and snatch them up. Some biggie-wiggies high up in companies like to prepare their underlings before a meeting by assigning them topics to research before the meeting. Steal away such assignments before they get a chance to see them, and they look like fools, plus the meeting becomes a waste of time.

It can be helpful to make use of an inside connection to the company. They can help bring up certain topics, like false trends that can be sold to executives eager to make easy money with the latest hot ideas (but which really serve as a red herring from legitimate business); or poor business ideas that can entangle them, to further misapply corporate energies. Or they can simply stand up and filibuster.

A meeting is good if it wastes a lot of time. A meeting is *better* if it continues wasting time long after the meeting has ended. You want to create meetings that will lead to lots of useless follow-up work. If you have any contact with people in the meeting you would want them to introduce lots of sticking points into discussions; raise lots of questions about problems with the firm that need to be addressed by multiple people in several departments. Think of all the inter-department battles that will ensure! Another way to make meetings last longer is to get your hands on the minutes of the previous meeting (which you'll find from your previous searching through computer files). Introduce indecipherable typos into the minutes, things that don't make sense, or actual mistakes. (Like if Jane was supposed to take care of an action item, change it to Sally.) As the minutes are read back, there will be much useless discussion, debate, and wonderment at exactly what transpired during that last meeting, and whether the note-taker is qualified to take minutes at all.

Attack #76. Act Like Miss Unmanners

Suppose you find out about an off-site meeting where the participants have never met before, but are soon to meet at a hotel or conference room, or at another company's office. A sales rep from your company is meeting with a potentially big new customer, let's say. Or some trainers from your company are going to perform a seminar to build customer loyalty. Handle this lucky turn of events by doing a two-step. Step 1 is to cancel the meeting, seminar, training session, or appointment with the customer. And step 2 is go yourself to the canceled meeting, and wreck it for the company.

First call or fax the executive at your firm and tell them you'd like to reschedule for the next day. Another way to do it is to call the businessman, pretend you're the assistant, and say you're sorry to change plans last minute but your boss told you a new address for the meeting. Give the businessman an address across town at the local whorehouse — and be ready for cameras to photograph the event!

Of course the guy he was supposed to meet with has no idea of this postponement and is sitting there waiting for your company to show up. That's where you come in — literally.

You head off to the meeting with the client. You take the place of the real meeting participant, and exhibit the kind of behavior that will lose you the sale. (Subtlely racist or anti-Semitic, or sexist comments, depending on the make and model of the other attendees.) Quote prices too high. Say you're sorry but business has been so bad you can't take on any new clients until you're done with litigation and lawsuits. Or maybe come to an agreement that the company could never agree to. No matter what happens, no matter how it turns out, you end up making the company look foolish, and the customers or potential partner loses all faith in the company.

Attack #77. Shake It Up

There are plenty of ways to shake up that meeting, distract the participants, and ensure the meeting gets off to a bad start — and continues down a sour path to a very destructive end. Make sure you create a lot of noise outside so they can't hear each other, slip the waiter some bucks to spill a coffee on one of them, or if it's a night meeting, park your car in the parking lot so the headlamps shine brightly into the conference room.

As your industrial espionage unfolds you will undoubtedly find schedules on secretaries' computers, detailing all the "whens" and "whats" of their next meeting. The memo shown earlier in Attack #74 (Food) offers the seeds needed to rain on their parade. They've listed exactly which equipment they require, so you'll know specifically what to look out for to mess up their plans. Times, dates, and places are all clearly marked. Break times are handy to have so you'll know when to hang out near the smokers, to overhear their conversations. Departure times are useful to note in schedules. That way you'll know when it's time to vacate the parking lot after messing with their cars.

On other computers in that same office I found letters to restaurants ordering dinner parties for a particular date and time. These letters often indicate everything from what foods will be prepared, to the credit card information, to names of people who will be attending. You can think of many ways of causing each of these meetings to run afoul if only you have this little bit of information that you glean from these memos.

On someone's computer you might find minutes of a meeting. Minutes might include notes on when and where future meetings will be held, and who attends these meetings. Then you'll know more about it, so the next time they have that meeting you will be prepared to infiltrate it (or infiltrate the empty offices of the people attending). If it was a marketing meeting you might find out information on planned marketing events, where advertising will be placed, costs, pitfalls, and trouble spots they are looking into. Minutes often include action notes, what actions various people are to take, which shows the direction they are heading and what problems weigh on their minds.

Attack #78. Induce Inventory

This attack can be devastating, especially to newer companies. Put on your most impressive business suit and pose as a buyer for whatever they're selling. Print up quality letterhead and business cards, and go in as someone who's out to give the company millions of bucks. Engage in meetings with them, many meetings, express your great interest. In fact, your goal should be to induce them to step up their production as much as possible. Premature inventory buildup is an incredibly common mistake, and extremely costly too.

Even better is if you can persuade the company to design a new product specifically for your imagined firm. If the money offer is high enough, they may get to work on it (but make sure it's a product few others would want). This happened at a software company I worked at, where another firm offered the company president big bucks to develop a specialty product just for them. The agreement was that our company would be able to sell the product after it was developed. So! Massive amounts of people-energy went into creating this thing, thus diverting key people away from the company's main purpose in life. When the product was finally finished our company did receive the agreed-upon compensation, but few regular customers wanted it, thus it had hardly been worth the effort. The mistake made was one of the most common mistakes in business: not adequately testing a product to see what the demand is. No demand means no customers, means no money in the company's pockets.

Attack #79. Foul Up Their Focus Groups

"Focus Groups are people who are selected on the basis of their inexplicable free time and their common love of free sandwiches," explains cartoonist and business satirist Scott Adams. "They are put in a room and led through a series of questions by a trained moderator. For many of these people it will be the first time they've ever been fed and listened to in the same day."[2] Now focus groups aren't all free sandwiches and fun, however, for serious company-screwing-up can also go on there. If you can weasel your way into a focus group or gabfest of some kind in which company representatives lend you their ears, you can be sure to fill up aforementioned ears with a lot of bullcrap. (Same goes for warranty cards, marketing surveys, Internet questionnaires and any other chance you have to lay out your opinions to the company.) Give them plenty of wrong info about your likes and dislikes. Send them in wrong directions by making tacky suggestions. If they hear enough of it they might end up making a big costly mistake.

Guy Kawasaki writes about a little scam he pulled in this regard to help his fledgling software company. *Macworld* magazine held a contest each year to pick the best computer products. Kawasaki sent letters and ballots to all his customers, asking them to *pleeeeeeeeeease* vote for his software. They did. And they won the vote. And they even pissed off Microsoft in the process. With a little ha-ha in his voice, Kawasaki notes: "We won the award, but 'stuffing' the ballot box was more fun. Our actions did not involve falsifying ballots from fictitious people. We simply encouraged our own customers to vote for our product — mobilizing a group of satisfied users. It's not my fault that Microsoft didn't think of this."[3] You may not be as honorable as Kawasaki, so you might indeed take some of the additional unethical steps he advises against. And I'm sure it will be just as fun.

Citations

1. Peppers, Don. *Life's a Pitch Then You Buy.* Currency Doubleday. New York. 1995. pp. 8-11. Peppers' book starts with some tales of cocky stunts he and his boys have played out.
2. Adams, Scott. *The Dilbert Principle: A Cubicle's Eye View of Bosses, Meetings, Management Fads & Other Workplace Afflictions.* HarperCollins. New York. 1996. p. 139. Sage business advice interspersed with cartoons.
3. Kawasaki, George. *How to Drive Your Competition Crazy: Creating Disruption for Fun and Profit.* pp. 188-189.

Travel

Executives are always taking trips away from the office. Salespeople are usually out on the road, on the runway, in a hotel, or at a train depot. Trips are very important to many businesses. It's important that the trip is meaningful, worth the money spent on airfare, hotel, food, taxi cabs, entertainment, transporting product, and all the rest of it. Lots of big bucks are being spent. The company wouldn't spend that much if it didn't think it would make it back in increased revenues, new prospects, or more product sales. Therefore if you can derail a business trip, not only are you wasting lots of money for the company, you're also costing them tons of money and sales down the road! The attacks in this section focus on how you can make sure the company wastes as much of its money as possible on travel, while getting as little return as possible on their investment.

If you've followed the advice in the preceding sections, you've gotten inside the company, looked through their computer files and schedulers, and so you know exactly who is going on business trips, and where they will be going. Here is an example of a computer file I found in the word processor of a sales rep's secretary:

Mark's Travel Itinerary

Friday, October 30
Lv Laguardia: 8:00 a.m.
American Flt. 553
Arr. O'Hare: 9:26 a.m.

Sunday, November 1
Lv O'Hare: 8:00 p.m. American Flt. 554
Arr. Laguardia: 10:59 p.m.

Hilton Towers
Check-in: Friday, October 30
Check-out: Sunday, November 1

Requested early check-in October 30 through Barbara in Reservations.

I've found dozens of files like this on the computer systems of secretaries, administrative assistants, and their ilk. The assistant prints it out and gives it to the executive so he'll know what he's doing the next few days. She keeps a copy for herself so she can make sure the trip proceeds smoothly.

In another office, another file I found included these instructions and more:

Before Ted's trip, ask JoAnn who is picking up Ted at the airport when he arrives. Call that person and confirm with them Ted's arrival flights and his departure flights (they're on the calendar). Ask that person for their home number, car phone number and/or cell phone number. Tell that person Ted wants the numbers in case his flight is delayed and he needs to reach him/her.

A quick trip through the Rolodex found JoAnn's number, and now I or any industrious spy with a good phone personality had the ability to find out a whole lot of information about any of executive Ted's big business trip plans.

Now suppose you were snooping around and you found some files like that (or you found a listing in a scheduler program). What should you do with it? Try these attacks:

Attack #80. Help Them Miss Their Plane

First, try to find the plane tickets. The secretary might have them, or the executive might. If you can find the tickets and switch them for phonies, you can take the plane yourself, or (less dangerous) find some sap to board the airplane with the real tickets.

In any case you know exactly when his flight leaves and arrives, thus you know exactly where this executive will be at those times — at the airport, or on the way to the airport.

Frank's Limousine Service Inc.
69 Applesauce Lane
Chummy, PA 08801

Dear Frank's Limousine:

Following is my list of pick-ups covering the period from Monday, February 5th to Friday February 9th.

Stellar Stapler Company has a billing account set up with Frank. Please charge this account and send the bill for all these transfers to my attention at the above address.

Call me if you have any questions.

Sincerely,

(signed)
2/5-Mon

Daniel Danes
From: Newark Airport
To: Hyatt Regency Hotel
Flight: Continental Express #3615 arriving at 2:03 p.m.

2/5-Mon
Stephen Daedelus
From: Newark Airport
To: Hyatt Regency Hotel
Flight: United #852 arriving at 9:58 p.m.

2/6-Tues
Helen Founds
From: Newark Airport
To: Hyatt Regency Hotel
Flight: Northwest #770 arriving at 10:55 a.m.

2/7-Wed
Laticia Feeney
From: LaGuardia Airport
To: Hyatt Regency Hotel
Flight: Air Canada Flg #704 arriving at 10:22 a.m.

Another useful computer file you might find is like the one shown above. This letter was followed by a two-page list of salespeople, detailing when they should be picked up from their homes and brought to the airport. The list also gave flight information and their home addresses. There are any number of ways to send them off course. You could send your own car to pick them up at the office. You might call the cab or limo company and cancel the order they've put in for cars. Or you might be able to intercept the travel arranger's memo before it ever reaches the executives in the first place.

Help them miss their plane, and that business trip will be off to a really bad start. Especially considering that you'll follow that up by infiltrating their limo (Attack #82) and meetings (Attack #76). But if you can't botch up their plane travel, you can at least follow them on their way, as the next attack describes...

Attack #81. Play Follow the Executive

Once you've gotten travel details such as those described above, you have a prime opportunity to catch an executive or salesperson (or several of them) out of their element. You can be waiting for them at the airport, at the hotel, or wherever their itinerary tells you they will be. Travelers usually walk around like zombies enveloped in an exhausted daze, in unfamiliar locations, out in public away from the safety and comfort of home. For these reasons it makes it somewhat easier to walk away with someone else's laptop computer, suitcase, or briefcase. Be especially on the lookout for opportunities to walk off with your mark's stuff in airport waiting areas, restrooms, registration desks, ticket counters, screening areas, and curbside check-in areas. It's helpful to work your ruse with a helper. One person distracts with questions and conversation, while the other one steals his notebook computer or briefcase. If you've done a thorough tailing job you'll even know what his baggage looks like, and might be able to pull it off the luggage carousel before he gets there. He will be left in a vulnerable and helpless predicament as he must then go about the rest of his business trip unprepared.

Attack #82. The Limousine Scheme

The calendar says he will be greeted by a limo at the airport to take him to the hotel. So you call one of your cronies who lives in that city, have him dress up in a suit, and take the executive's place in the limousine. The executive is left bewildered and stranded.

There may be other side benefits as well. Some busy executives have their assistants pre-pack the limo with business items to attend to on the drive to the airport, so you'll have full access to all of that.

Since your friend has hijacked the company's rented limo, it's his job to tip the limo driver. You have three options:

1. Don't tip him. This one seems most obvious, but make sure you let the driver know exactly what company you're with so he thinks bad of the company, and might even tell all his friends how terrible it is.

2. Tip him with petty cash you stole from the firm. If the company is a localized or specialized one, where the limo driver's patronage wouldn't matter much, then you might as well tip him — not with your own money of course. Do it with money you've taken from the corporate piggy bank.

3. Tip him with confidential info on stocks you gleaned from your spying. And if you've really got some hot information that works against the company, be sure to let it out of the bag. We don't want that company's stock prices rising!

Maybe the limo was taking the guy from the airport directly to his first meeting. Then you should go to the meeting and disrupt it. Also remember to cancel his hotel accommodations so if the real guy ever shows up he'll be out of luck and stranded on the sidewalk without a comfy bed to collapse into.

Attack #83. Invade Their Hotel Room

People are vulnerable when they're away from home. Even though a hotel is supposed to serve as one's home away from home, they are still vulnerable. The traveler does not have easy access to all the things that one uses in everyday life, from socks and shoes, to medicines, computer disks, research material, electronic equipment, toiletries, and all the other stuff that goes into a life. Therefore, if you can ruin, steal, borrow, or mess up any of these things while the person is on-the-road, the effect is heightened. Can't find socks at home, no big deal, just pull some from the hamper. Can't find socks you thought you packed in your suitcase, and it becomes a small crisis. You don't know where to shop, how to get there, or whether the price you're paying is reasonable (it's probably three times the cost you would've paid at home for the same item).

So let's say you've got some target executive from the company, and you know he's on a business trip and staying at some hotel. You might have found this out from the research activities we discussed earlier (snooping). You might have to tail him from the airport to the hotel to see what room he ends up in. Sneak into his hotel room, somehow or other, while he's away conducting business.

Maybe you can scam the front desk clerk to get a key. If the hotel uses those reprogrammable magnetic cards, find one lying around, run it through a magnet, then go up to the desk and say, "I can't get into my room, room 503, what's wrong with this stupid card thing!" They have enough trouble with stupid assholes who accidentally reprogram their card, so they won't bother arguing with you. They'll simply reprogram the card so you can get back into your room.

Another way is to wait till he's out of the room. Keep putting the maid service sign on his door so the maids know it's okay to come in. (A side benefit is he'll be constantly disturbed when they barge in when he's there.) When the maid comes in, confidently stride in yourself, smile hello at her and say you have to get something — which you do.

While on the road they will have with them some crucial equipment and supplies:

- product samples
- laptop computers
- executive organizer
- address book/calendar

Steal any of this stuff and it will seriously screw him up, plus you can use the information you gather to interfere with his appointments, presentations, meetings, and so on.

While in the room eat and drink everything in the mini bar. Install bugs if you've got them. Change the alarm clock or travel clock from a.m. to p.m. He won't notice. So now when he sets the alarm to 6 a.m. it will wake him at 6 p.m. and he'll be seriously late. Plug in the coffee machine, turn it on, and let it churn away.

If you see anything laying around let the gears in your head whir a while and you'll figure a way to exploit it. Find a PostIt note with a phone number to call, and you can change some digits to make it undialable. The number 1 can become a 4 or 7, 2s become 3s. Or rip a very obvious hole in his only good suit, thus causing great embarrassment when he has to meet with that important client that night. You might find his one pair of comfortable shoes and make off with them, forcing him to stand around all day at the trade show in his stiffer and harder dress shoes. Take return airline tickets. I'm sure once you gain access to the room you'll have barrels of fun monkeying around with whatever you find in there.

Attack #84. Listen In

While he's on the road he will do business dinners. Try to get the next table and listen close to the conversation. Farfetched? Think again. Scott Clark, a manager at an electronics company described two instances of accidental eavesdropping where he heard *himself* being discussed! Clark stopped into a coffee shop before meeting with some managers of another company — and he overheard them discussing the negotiation strategy they were going to use against him. On another occasion he was riding the Metroliner from New York to Washington when he overheard competitors talking over their strategy to beat him out of an upcoming contract.[1] Both of these were casual accidents, so imagine what you can accomplish if you specifically set out to overhear the enemy talking.

So there you are in the restaurant, a table away from the representative of that loathsome company as he meets with a potential customer. Your target gets up to go to the bathroom. Aha, opportunity! Now you can say things to the customer in the guy's absence. "Psst... That guy looks amazingly like that suspected child molester in the paper — say, is he from Company Corporation in Dallas, Texas?" (Of course he is!) Or, if you're not theatrical enough to do that, simply say it at your own table, loud enough for the guy at the next table to hear.

If there is an accessible coat room, look in your target's coat pocket for interesting items, also look in the client's pocket. If the client has your target's business card in his pocket get rid of it. It will then be slightly more difficult for him to contact him again.

Attack #85. Use Corporate Policy Against Them

Earlier we talked about cultivating insiders to help unravel the company. You'll be especially lucky if your insiders have the opportunity to travel at corporate expense. Make sure they keep all receipts and produce an unarguably itemized expense report of the journey so the company will be throwing away as much money as possible on travel. Naturally your insider will not make any efforts to secure the cheapest flight, the cheapest meal, or the cheapest hotel room. Some companies foolishly encourage this behavior. The story is told of one savvy entre-preneur who guiltily booked himself an expensive $740 coach fare, and met some friends at the airport who were working for his former company, and had taken business-class tickets for $3,950. The friends later explained that corporate policy prevented them from buying first class tickets, but they were entitled to business-class even when it made absolutely no business sense. The entrepreneur walked away smiling, because:

> He realized that he had been freed forever from any attempts at such childish greed — a greed born of a need for revenge against a company you didn't really enjoy working for. "The company's policy!" What a battle cry of revenge by those who felt ill-used by the corporate system.[2]

Now *that's* the kind of attitude that you're looking for! That's the kind of attitude with which you wish to imbue the workforce of your target company, and that you wish to exploit to its full advantage. One hopes that your insiders, and all whom they can persuade to follow in their footsteps, manage to take everything that's offered to them, even when — especially when — it doesn't make business sense.

Citations

1. AT&T Security. *The Security Seven: Your Guide to Protecting AT&T's Treasures.* p. 6.
2. Gill, Michael and Sheila Paterson. *Fired Up!: From Corporate Kill-off to Entrepreneurial Kick-Off.* Viking, Penguin Group. New York. 1996. pp. 39-40.

Trade Show Tactics

Trade shows cost tons of money. A mid-sized booth can cost $40,000 and larger booths can go for $250,000 or (way) up plus hotel, rental cars, setup time, meals, and more. Many companies attend three to six trade shows a year.[1] As it is, most trade shows are big wastes of money for companies. Here are some more numbers that one wonders how they dug up and how accurate they are: The Center for Exhibition Industry Research in Bethesda, Maryland, says 54 percent of trade show exhibitors fail to set objectives for trade show participation; and of the ones who do set goals, only half follow through.[2] It's also reported that most corporations surveyed said they don't bother even talking to people who pass by their exhibits. Why'd they bother paying all that money if they're not going to take advantage of their presence there? They might as well not be there at all. Given statistics like these, it's likely the company is already making a financial fool of itself on its own. By infiltrating trade shows you will ensure it is profitless for them.

Attack #86. Trash Their Booth

It's tiring work setting up a trade show booth. Too bad you're going to have to ruin it for them. If possible, sneak into the convention center before it opens to the public. If you put your mind to it (and set your alarm clock) you can probably tiptoe in a lot earlier than anyone from the booth will be there. Especially if you do this on the second or third night of the show, after they've been out all night socializing.

To sneak into the trade show, dress as if you are working a booth: Wear khakis and a trade show shirt. Wear the company button or pin you plucked from someone's desk (Attack #47), and carry a heavy carton with the company's logo on it. Hold the carton up over your chest (where your official trade show badge is supposed to be hanging). The guard won't question you at all, and if she does, just say you left your admissions badge inside the booth. Do this on the first day and you'll be surrounded by massive confusion (good). Or you might be able to get in the day before the show opens. In any case, go early in the morning. Now you're in the building before most other people.

Trash their booth. Throw away literature. Steal essential computer cables, the cables from audio systems, and signs. Unplug light bulbs. Look underneath curtained tables where product may be kept (or computer CPUs). Delete contents of hard drives. Pour honey on their keyboards. Destroy promotional video tapes.

Go in with a buddy on this one, so you can take turns trashing the booth and standing guard, in case someone from the company comes by. Of course if you've really done your homework (and a lot of snooping back at the home office) you'll know exactly which hotel and where the rats are sleeping, so you can post someone by their hotel room door and know exactly when they've arisen and are coming down to the show.

One pre-show wreck mess probably won't be enough to satisfy your lust for muss. At lunchtime the booths are often empty or less-well-staffed, which offers the chance to make a second hit-and-run attack. (Or third, or fourth...) These follow-up sabotages will ensure that you get them when they're down, never fully give them a chance to recover, and they will be standing on unstable ground throughout the entire trade show experience.

Attack #87. Make Them Play Follow the Leader

A major goal of trade shows is coming up with new sales prospects, so anything you can do to stymie that goal is like money down the toilet for them. Some companies put out a fish bowl, or hat, or box, or whatever, to catch business cards of customers who wish to receive more information on the company. Naturally you'll want to do some fishing in that bowl and take out any cards that might actually lead to sales. Drop in handfuls of phony cards, or cards that you carefully picked out from various places that you're sure will have no interest in buying from that company. Drop in cards of competitors. Boy won't the sales reps be disheartened when they start cold-calling and find they can't get barely a glimmer of interest, let alone a sale.

Companies sometimes put out questionnaires or surveys, often with a contest attached to it. Same thing applies here; grab legitimate surveys and replace them with forged ones. If you snuck in before the show, it should be easy to grab blank forms. Fill them out that night, and come back tomorrow to slyly drop them in the tank. All the effort they spend typing up and analyzing these surveys will be a meaningless waste of time.

Attack #88. Divert Their Attentions

Every moment that trade show booth is being rented by the firm, it's costing them a fortune. That's why you want to divert their attention away from any profit-making activities in that booth. Organize your cohorts to wander into the booth at various times throughout the day to talk to them so no legitimate customers can get through. Take up their time by asking lots of technical, hard-hitting and difficult questions about their products or company history. (If any real customers overhear them it will look bad.) Make them feel bad; wear them down. Have them demonstrate and demonstrate the product to the point of annoyance. Also, while they give a demonstration in front of an audience, you can heckle it, ask unfair questions to which they have no ready answers, or point out that they're just putting on a show.

"Let's see some real-world use of the product, not just this polished trade-show bull."

"Why don't you have this feature?"

"Why is your Tacoma office being investigated by the Department of Justice?"

"Who at your company is responsible for product safety? There are some problems I'd like him to address."

"Why are you all white males here, huh?"

Get different people on your team to ask difficult questions like these so it will look like random barrages of headaches rather than one person out for vengeance. Potential customers and journalists will espy with a mixture of voyeuristic glee and embarrassment that the company can provoke such negative reactions from the crowd.

Attack #89. Play With Their Heads

Trade shows may be one of the few places you can actually meet and greet with company insiders. Use that to your advantage as you scout out the weak people links in the business. You're always on the lookout for employees who explode easily, who don't truly understand the product, or are rude — and then exploit that facet of them. Make a federal case out of it.

Claim you want to make a big order then don't — demoralize them. You can arrange to meet later to buy, then stand them up. Better yet, tell them you've decided to go with a competitor.

At some trade shows you're not allowed to sell products. If they violate that rule, fink on them. Pretend to be from a rival company and complain of their unfair practices. Fax a letter to their home office on falsified letterhead warning them they are violating their contract by selling at the convention. That'll give them a good scare. The more you can worry the people manning the booth, the less effective they'll be at making sales and sealing deals with real customers.

A trade show is a good place to spread rumors too, about the company and their competition. To discourage them, let it slip that their rivals are doing much better across the way. In short, you want to engage in psychological warfare against anyone associated with that company at the trade show, whether they be sales people, or customers. When in doubt, psych them out.

Attack #90. Talk Your Way Into Information

While the trade show is in full swing, hop over to your target's booth and find a non-sales person, like an engineer or programmer, and start asking technical questions about the product. You can use the ruse of one oily legal counsel who coached his company employees to wear customers' name badges when attending trade shows, so competitors will speak more freely as they salivate over the impending sale they hope to make.[3] Even if you don't resort to deception, technical types love talking about technical matters, and programmers love bragging about all the sweat equity that went into their babies, so you're sure to come out of the convo with tons of confidential insider knowledge about their products. While you're in the booth, make sure you get an eyeful of all the new gizmos and whatsajigs they're promoting for sale, for you never know how the knowledge will help your cause. At one product showing, a company found a competitor's representative wearing out his pen taking notes on all sorts of stuff in their exhibits. The man confessed this was the third time he'd visited the exhibit, fed his R&D team with information and sketches, and they'd sent him back to learn more, more, and more.[4] Obviously companies don't realize the competitive value of the information they often make publicly available.

Attack #91. Attend Speeches

Try to stay awake now. At trade shows and the like, they always have speeches, lectures, seminars. See if you can attend any of that. Guy Kawasaki, former bright boy for Apple Computer, points out that the excitement of trade shows, conferences, and association meetings can loosen lips: "Most people like to impress the audience at these kinds of events, and may leak information to do so." Kawasaki advises executives hoping to find out the inside scoop on their rivals: "Listen to the speeches of your competition's management to learn about its strategic direction. Be sure to shop your competition's booths at shows."[5]

Top executives are often incredibly prepared when getting up on stage. They might be briefed beforehand on what questions are likely to be asked, and how they should answer those questions. If you can locate those prepared questions and answers on an assistant's computer or files you will have "psychic knowledge" of what all his answers will be to any given question. Dream up arguments against them. Think up tough questions that aren't answered on the briefing sheet. Poke holes in those answers — then challenge him with your hole pokers!

Citations

1. Conlon, Ginger. "Making Trade Shows Pay Off" in *Sales & Marketing Management*. January 1996. p. 90. Statistics on trade shows.
2. Conlon, Ginger. "Trade Show Tsk, Tsks" in *Sales & Marketing Management*. November 1995. p. 96. Stats on trade shows objectives.
3. Washington Researchers Publishing, *How Competitors Learn Your Company's Secrets*. p. 10.
4. *Ibid.*, p. 10.
5. Kawasaki, George. *How to Drive Your Competition Crazy: Creating disruption for fun and profit*. Hyperion. New York. 1995. p. 49.

Retail Stores and Showrooms

So you're set against some retail shop, grocery store, car dealership, lemonade stand, clothing boutique, bakery, or some other shop in your neighborhood? Good news — you may be in luck. If you work hard, you've got a good shot at taking it down using the attacks in this section. Retail stores are pretty easy to get jobs in, hence easier to attack from the inside. Also many employees of local stores are miscreant teenagers who won't mind getting even with their boss. Here are some attacks to get you started.

Attack #92. Human Barriers

Use various tactics to persuade every bum, hobo, smelly vagrant, crackhead, and ornery type to loiter in front of or inside the store. This will discourage legitimate customers and be a nuisance to the owner and employees.

- Spread the word or hand out flyers — the store offers freebies to homeless people. Or let them know that it's a particularly easy store to steal from.

- You can always bribe some drunken bums to stand in front. Encourage them to barf.

- Ask unruly leather-clad denizens to stand there and bother incoming customers by playing "bouncer."

- Stand outside the store yelling, "They ripped me off!" Tell all passers-by about the bait-and-switch operation they run there. (If it's a legitimate complaint, tell the FTC about it.)

- Another idea is make a fake ad or hand out flyers promising free baby formula, diapers and other childcare products to moms. This will fill up the store with crying, screaming babies — not to mention all the crying, screaming mothers getting into arguments with the cashiers over their allegedly "free" products.

I like the free coupon idea because it screws the store both ways. If they do accept the coupon then they're losing money. But if they don't accept it, they create ill feelings towards their store. Either way you win, they lose.

Attack #93. Get the Scoop

Shoplifting is a major threat to most retail businesses and the more shoplifting you can do, the closer to the grave that store will be. Shoplifting's more costly than most people realize, because the loss is more than just the value of the stolen item. The retailer actually loses the cost of the item, plus the profit that would have resulted from a sale. Suppose a $10 item is stolen, so ten bucks go down the hole. But the store would have made some profit on that. Let's say the store normally makes a 5% profit on items sold (so it would have made 50¢ on the sale). Not much profit is made on each sale, so the store has to sell $210 worth of merchandise to recoup its loss of $10.50 on the stolen item.[1]

- Approach employees who look like they can be trusted and ask if they know a way to steal stuff from the store. They'll know all the inside tricks, like the hole in the back fence that they pass stuff through to their buddies.

- If you can, sneak into the back areas of the store. Usually there are no cameras, and there's probably a back exit. You can take more from the back areas, without fear of being caught, than you can from the actual sales floor.

- Another way to do this is to switch price tickets from one item to another. If the price is ticketed on the caps or lids, perhaps you can switch the lids of a lower-priced item and a higher-priced one. You walk out the store with the higher-priced item having paid the lower price.

- You might be able to convince the store to give you a refund on goods you haven't purchased. The simple way is to merely pick an item off the shelf, and bring it to the return desk claiming it was a gift that you'd like to return. If you're more savvy you'll first scout out the store and parking lot for discarded receipts. Now you don't have to "lie" and say it was a gift — show them your receipt to "prove" you bought it there yourself!

- Give employees the idea that their employer owes them something more than just their paycheck. After all, don't they sometimes come in to work a little early, or stay a little late? Don't they get a lot more bullshit than their paycheck compensates them for? Why not distribute flyers near the store promoting this attitude, the way Bible-thumpers distribute flyers promoting the word of God?

- If you can team up with a cashier there are plenty of ways to move merchandise out of the store without paying full price for it. The cashier can ring up only part of a purchase, and pocket the rest; or not ring it up at all; or give refunds when refunds are not due; or simply walk out with it; or throw it in the trash can, to be retrieved later after the can is emptied in the dumpster behind the store.

- Find out what procedures are like at the store for returns, replacements, broken items, switches, and paying by check — either by asking, observing, or getting a job at the store. You will soon discover there is a way to beat the system or break the rule. There usually is. I know at stores where I've worked it's always been possible for someone cocky enough to get refunds for items that weren't purchased at the store, or to buy merchandise with a bad check, and in general to cheat the store out of money in various ways. But it all hinges on having the knowledge of the policies of that store.

- A full-scale burglary might also be arranged. It's said that a theft can cause a store to lose an *entire year's worth of profit*.[2] And even if their insurance covers some of that loss, their insurance costs might increase, and they have to pay the deductible anyway.

Music stores sometimes hold CDs in plastic cases. I've been able to do damage by using a pocket knife to rip open the case and take the CD inside. Some retail stores uses stickers that attach to the packaging. Either peel off the sticker or remove the item from its packaging before stealing. Book stores often sprinkle several electronic tags throughout a book. Make sure you check an item thoroughly for multiple tags before walking off with it. In some cases you can empty the contents of a high-priced item into a lower-priced item, then pay the lower price.

Clothing stores often electronically tag merchandise. Usually they squirt you with ink if you're not careful. I've been able to cleanly remove those tags in the comfort of my own home, but under pressure in a store it would probably be very difficult to do so. Since your goal is merely to harm the store and not to wear the clothing, why not use scissors to cut off the cloth around the tags before shoplifting the garments. Take several garments into the dressing room with you and do your dirty work away from the prying eyes of the camera. Sometimes an attendant will count merchandise as you enter the dressing room. To fool the attendant, simply hide smaller garments inside a larger shirt or pants. In the dressing room you can layer your clothes, with the stolen merchandise underneath your own clothing.

Professional shoplifters have been using the "booster bag" more and more, which unfortunately is making it more well-known among store security guards and police. A booster bag is a shopping bag that's lined with foil. Stolen items are placed in the bag, and the foil stops the electronic sensors from sensing that the item is being brought out.

It may be safer to simply look for an employee exit you can leave through. There are generally no sensors back there to detect your stolen merchandise. I've walked out many employee exists and nobody cares. Remember, most stores are staffed by teenagers who, even if they care, will be too intimidated to confront you. Some stores have attached restaurants or coffee shops which don't have sensors hooked up, even when the main entrance does.

Oh, by the way, if you get caught, don't blame me. Who was the one dumb enough to try this?

📖 *How to Steal Food From the Supermarket* by J. Andrew Anderson. Loompanics Unlimited, Port Townsend, Washington. 1993. Contains a great many more ideas on how you can rip off a food store.

📖 *Cut Your Losses!* by Keith O'Brien. International Self-Counsel Press Ltd. Bellingham, Washington. 1996. A great overview of every kind of scam, con, rip-off, fraud, and means of losing money that retail shops face. If you're a business owner, this offers lots of fine advice on keeping the books healthy and the registers balancing. If you're a business wrecker, gives many ideas in that regard too.

■■■■■■■■■■■

Attack #94. Shoplift Their Shopping Carts

Shopping carts cost about $100 each, which makes them one of the most important items for your shoplifting endeavors. The more you steal, the more money the store loses. Think how many loaves of bread they'll have to sell to equal just one stolen shopping cart. The trouble with making off with the things is you can't pop 'em in your pocket, and they don't fit easily into most cars.

• Your attack might have to be gradual, rolling away one or two carts per day, finding a nearby repository for them, such as over the side of an embankment, or in a neighboring garbage bin.

- If the carts are nondescript, try to leave them in the area of a competing store, which will benefit from your target store's loss.

- Are the carts left out at night? That's why bolt cutters were invented. Snap off the locks and chains, and free those silver chariots from their bonds.

- If you can't steal them all, at least cut off all the seat belts, deface the advertising, leave wads of sticky gum on the seats, and snip the metal in strategic places to leave sharp metal edges. Perhaps you can also fuss with the wheels until they're ready to fall off or don't turn at all.

A 1988 report on supermarket costs revealed that most stores have approximately one cart for every $1,000 in weekly business. You can use this rough estimate to figure out how much dough your target store is raking in annually — and step up your efforts to annihilate them accordingly.

Attack #95. Miracle on Dirty Tricks Street

Attacking a department store? Bribe their Santa Claus or Easter Bunny — or hell, try to get the job yourself — and lure kids and parents away to a competing store. In the movie *Miracle on 34th Street* this tactic worked in the store's favor, but you can put a nasty spin on it. Tell the kids this store is all out of the goodies they seek, and they should tell their parents to leave immediately and shop across the street. Or whisper to the parents how much cheaper it is downtown, or for that matter you might want to let out a few well-chosen racist or sexist or pedophilic comments to scare away the parents from this disgusting store.

Attack #96. Screw Up Their Slotting

Manufacturers shell out big bucks to stores for "slotting" expenses. Originally slotting fees were created by store managers who were pissed off that companies were extending their brands out to infinity. It doesn't cost a food company much to sell the same cereal with ten different flavors and ten different boxes, but it sure drives the shelvers crazy as they stock and restock and push cartons around.[3] The stores said, hey, if they're going to overcrowd our shelf space, let's charge them for it. And so slotting was born. What may have started with good intentions has been quite a money maker for retail stores, and as the practice has become more accepted in the industry, stores abuse the privilege for all it's worth.

How much money are manufacturers paying per store? How much can a store expect to earn from slotting allowances? No one will say. But Pat Collins, president of Ralph's, a 127-store chain in southern California, told *USA Today* that his company spent $20 million in 1990 adding 10,000 new products and dropping 7,000. He said slotting allowances covered about 60 percent of the cost. A little simple mathematics tells us that companies paid Ralph's about $12 million in slotting allowances. Divide that by 127 stores and you get $94,000 per store.[4]

Notice that in 1993 (and Staten probably wrote that a year or so earlier), no one was talking about slotting expenses, it was such an unacknowledged source of revenue in the business. A few years later all that's changed. Some reports cite slotting expenses of $5,000 to $25,000 per item, per store.[5] Some publishers even pay to have their books reviewed (favorably of course) in the brochures bookstores hand out every month.[6] Book publishers may pay Barnes & Noble $10,000 a month to have a book placed in a corrugated display at the front of a store. Three thousand dollars per title buys an endcap, a display at the end of an aisle; or $10,000 for the whole display. "Independent bookstores have cried foul, even filing lawsuits against a number of large publishers, who they say, unfairly favor the chains when doling out co-op money; unable to compete a number of chains have gone out of business."[7] Smaller bookstores just don't have the clout to ask for big bucks like the large chains demand. In short, they're forced to stay in business by merely *selling books*. That's fine if your competitors are also just selling books, but if your competitors are also getting paid what are essentially bribes by publishers to treat their books nicely, the smaller stores can't compete. One such chain was Endicott Booksellers in Manhattan which finally closed in the summer of 1995 because it finally couldn't keep up when these sorts of competitive games were being played by the big guns.[8]

- Mess up stuff in the store, put things in wrong aisles. Things that are supposed to be in eye-catching displays at the ends of aisles can be moved to less accessible places.

- Be sure to let the manufacturer or publisher know that their items, which they paid exorbitant slotting fees to be placed in certain spots, are being mishandled and misshelved by store employees. Cause animosity between the store and the businesses who rent store space from them.

- Fill up a cart of stuff, including lots of perishables, and leave it in the wrong place in back of the store. Do this on a regular basis to provide a constant source of headaches to employees. Watch out for security cameras and guards though.

- Things that are supposed to be at eye-level, move to the bottom shelf, or out of reach on the top shelf — or vice-versa. The staff might be more content to leave it there because they might not notice or don't want to rearrange it, and the people who pay for prime slot spots will be upset that their products end up out of reach on the top shelf.

Attack #97. Sidetrack the Supervisors

Get rid of the store owners and experienced managers, and the store will be left with inexperienced helpers — usually teenagers who gab a lot, don't get the job done, and may shoplift or overlook shoplifting. Divert the supervisors and then you can sneak in and do all sorts of things because the "hired help" aren't watching you. Or by casing the store you can learn when the supervisors take their lunch break, thus freeing up the store for mischievous activity. Store owners always lament about how they can't hire full-time sales clerks who know how to work the floor and make sales and keep order and control. "The problem is that when Bob and I are not around, not much work gets done and customer service suffers," said business owner Dolores. "We have some friends who shop the store at times when we're not there. They tell us that customers are often ignored while our employees gossip with each other. We have a store manager, but it doesn't seem to help. Maybe we need a new one."[9] Remember the earlier discussion on persuading employees to quit or be fired — that's easier to do with retail since no one's too committed to it anyway and the stakes are lower, but turnover still brings with it the same set of monetary concerns such as costs of hiring, training, mistakes, and lost customers.

Attack #98. Objections

If the store sells cigarettes, object to that — they're encouraging teens to smoke (cigarettes are big moneymakers for any business that sells them). If a toy store is your target, find objectionable toys — guns, cowboys and Indians (they're Native Americans, of course), candy cigarettes, toys with small parts that can be swallowed, or unsafe displays the store. I mentioned before the nightclub that was closed down after a lawsuit was brought against it by the township. A separate lawsuit was brought against it by neighborhood residents who objected to the loud noise, litter, and inadequate parking facilities. Parking was an issue because the parking lot was overstuffed with dozens of more cars than it was meant to hold. Neighboring businesses found themselves unwittingly providing parking spaces for the nightclub's denizens; and safety was a factor, as people had to cross a busy street to find free parking spaces. This business's very popularity was what ultimately did it in, as all these issues angered nearby residents. Finally the township and residents agreed to drop the lawsuit if the club would agree to lose its liquor license and shut down. Instead of a hopping nightclub, we now have a Chinese restaurant. Not that I have anything against noodles.

There are hundreds of local laws and ordinances which are enforced only occasionally, if at all. Do your research and you might be able to find several items to use against the company. Consider zoning laws; ordinances that govern the visual look and appeal of storefronts; licenses, such as a liquor license, business license, or permits to sell certain items; and minimum markup laws that set prices at a certain level. Some states require a pharmacy to be owned, at least in part, by a pharmacist, but a medical doctor is barred from owning one.[10] Another way to entrap the company in a legal entanglement is if the company can be portrayed as morally indecent. Bars, topless clubs, adult bookstores, and sex shops fall into this category. Townships have been known to severely hurt or even shut down businesses by enacting laws that forbid dancing in a bar, or that restrict on which streets bars or topless clubs can exist; or laws that force certain kinds of shops to keep within a certain distance of schools, or other shops of its kind. These kinds of laws can contribute to the downfall of a business, and in fact that nightclub I was talking about before was the impetus to a new ordinance in my neighborhood restricting the location of bars and nightclubs on that particular street.

Publicize and make the most of such objections. You can also contact the radio shows or TV shows with which the company advertises and explain why you oppose the business, and that you're boycotting the show — and oh yes, get your whole team involved on this one so they'll know you mean business.

Attack #99. Stage a Beer Run

This is a good one to work on convenience stores and other small food shops. Arrange for a group of your wildest friends to storm the store on a beer run. They run in en masse, ransack the place, grab whatever's in sight, and run out the door. Make sure they wear masks to obscure their faces from the omnipresent security cameras; and do this at an off-time, such as when there aren't any cops yakking and scarfing down snacks in the parking lot.

Attack #100. Location, Location, Screw Their Location

As we all know, location, location, location means everything in business, retail business usually, but other businesses as well. Case in point: A group of doctors noticed after six years their business was stagnant. Throughout that time they'd made sure to get to know their neighbors and make themselves visible in the community. Despite that, the practice was on a sour streak and not going anywhere. They pulled in a business consultant to help them. The consultant asked how many patients live or work within 3 or 4 blocks of the office? Being staunch Beemer guys themselves (I imagine), doctors who are used to having people make appointments to meet them, it never occurred to them that some people actually don't like being inconvenienced by a long drive, or that some people can't drive at all. Especially sick patients. So the doctors moved their office to where the patients were, and six months later — now get this — after six years of floundering they moved their offices and within six months *their business doubled.*[11] Moral: Attack their location any way you can.

• Their driveway may became mysteriously inaccessible when someone leaves a junked car there, or broken glass and rusty stabs of metal are scattered around the parking lot.

• A few crack vials dropped here and there in the vicinity, followed by an anonymous call to the police, and another call to the local papers, will make some people fear to visit the area.

• If someone claims to be raped or attacked in the parking lot or behind the store, it will certainly scare off many visitors.

• Bomb threats (and strange devices left lying around) can clear a store fast.

• Make it unpleasant for customers visiting the store, by throwing stink bombs, smoke bombs, playing obnoxious music nearby, and upturning trash barrels.

• Some businesses post signs far back from the store which help divert traffic into the place ("HOTEL 15 FEET AHEAD" or "FISH! 50 FEET FORWARD!"). Pull out the signs and destroy them. The business owners are not too likely to realize the signs are gone, and people will be less likely to pop into their place now that they're not forewarned about it.

Shopping centers and strip malls have their ups and downs, and after a while most fall out of favor with the shopping community as new stores spring up elsewhere. It's your job to help your target's shopping center to deteriorate a little faster than normal.

Attack #101. The Damage You Can Do

Here are some final additional ideas to wreck food stores and other retail shops:

- Unplug their ice machine or vending machines so the ice melts and food spoils.

- Maybe you can find a way to heat up their frozen foods? Squoosh their produce?

- Let loose an army of bugs in their bakery or produce section.

- Remove all coupons stuck onto the food so customers will be less prone to buy.

- Use a sharp razor blade to slice open a near-invisible slit down the sides of milk and juice cartons. It should only drip out a little, but when someone squeezes the container to pick it up, the contents will squirt out, creating a mess, and making the product unsellable.

- If you're really nervy, you and a bunch of friends can go in, spend a long time making selections of items throughout the store. Bring them all up to the counter, and after the cashier has rung them all up, announce you don't have the money after all, and walk out, leaving it all there in a pile to be reshelved.

- Smash the lights in the parking lot and snip the wires, creating a dark, scary environment. Customers, especially female customers, stay away from stores with potentially dangerous parking lots. Poor lighting encourages vandalism and break-ins, requires more security patrols, and makes it more difficult to remove snow and trash from the parking lot, in addition to the cost of repairing the lights. (One New York mall which improved its lighting increased profits and sales substantially, reduced vandalism almost entirely, and saved thousands of dollars in reduced security and faster refuse pick-up.)[12]

Citations

1. O'Brien, Keith. *Cut Your Losses!* International Self-Counsel Press Ltd. Bellingham, Washington. 1996. Math from p. 5. A great overview of every kind of scam, con, rip off, fraud, and means of losing money that retail shops face. If you're a business owner, this offers lots of fine advice on keeping the books healthy and the registers balancing. If you're a business wrecker, gives many ideas in that regard too.
2. *Ibid.*, p. 11.
3. Lucas, Allison. "Shelf Wars: High-Priced Space Leaves Entrepreneurs out of the Aisles" in *Sales & Marketing Management*. March 1996. p. 121. Short article on slotting fees in supermarkets and how they hurt small businesses.
4. Staten, Vince. *Can You Trust a Tomato in January?* Simon & Schuster. New York. 1993. Interesting anecdotes be-

hind-the-scenes on your neighborhood grocery store and the products within. Information on slotting from pp. 167-168.

5. Lucas. "Shelf Wars."
6. Tabor, Mary. "In Bookstore Chains, Display Space is for Sale" in *The New York Times.* January 15, 1996. pp. A1, D8. Complete exposé on the bookstore slotting controversy.
7. Burack, Sylvia K. "Roving Editor" in *The Writer.* June 1996. p. 4. The editor reports this month on the bookstore slotting controversy.
8. Tabor. p. D8.
9. Wright, Harold. *How to make 1,000 Mistakes in Business and Still Succeed: The Small Business Owners' Guide to Crucial Decisions,* p. 199.
10. Purpura, Philip. *Retail Security and Shrinkage Protection.* Butterworth-Heinemann. Boston. 1993. p. 31. Textbook-type book, but not dry and boring like some of these books are, on the problems that face retailers.
11. Wright. p. 75.
12. Purpura. p. 236.

Special Tactic Report:
Arson

Fire is frightening, and dangerous. More lives have been ruined by fire than most people care to believe. Fire consumes both people and property with an inhuman appetite for destruction that wants not to be quenched. Fire is a very powerful tool for putting corporations out of business.

A couple I know had their business destroyed by fire. They ran a food truck every weekend alongside a few other food trucks near a strip mall in upstate New York. They enjoyed doing it as a side business and were raking in a good amount of money off the books. One Sunday they came by and found the truck had been ravaged by fire. I believe the fire was started by jealous rival truck owners in the vicinity, but one never knows for sure. They didn't have the heart, nor the money, to start up the business again, so sadly they let the whole thing fold. One of the odd jobs which author David Sedaris had in his non-literary past was that of a wood stripper with a guy named Harry in Chicago; they brought tanks of "poisonous" chemicals into people's homes to strip their wood. But after doing this awhile, Sedaris writes, "Harry's truck caught fire, forcing him to close his business."[1] Dreams turn to ashes, one-two-three.

Fire can destroy buildings. Fire can destroy inventory, and stock for sale. Fire can destroy important papers, and expensive equipment. Fire can destroy working environments, like offices and cubicles.

No, I take that back. Probably nothing can destroy cubicles.

What Fire Investigators Look For

With a fire you've got two choices: Make it look like arson, or make it look like an accident. To make it look like an accident you'll have to know what the fire investigators are looking for when they investigate a fire. On the other hand, if you want it to look like arson, you might want to make it look like arson set by *someone in particular,* and certainly not by you.

Like reporters digging up a scoop, fire investigators want to know the who, what, when, where, why, and how of the fire. They have a need for information. If the arsonist can supply misleading answers to each of these questions, the investigators will happily take it all in and believe it. After all, they are detectives, and they are thrilled to believe they have unraveled the clues and solved the crime. Investigators know that most fires are accidents, and most crime is spur-of-the-moment. Therefore, if your very pre-meditated crime of arson is presented with realistic details that suggest an accident, or the actions of a pyromaniac employed by the firm, you will have created a believable mystery game for the investigators to play.

The origin points to an answer. The point of origin is the place where the fire began. The "point" may refer to a large area, such as an entire room, a localized area of the room ("in the supply closet") or a very restricted point in a localized area ("the pile of rags in the supply closet, where the cigarette fell"). In an accidental fire there is only one origin point, such as where a cigarette falls. But in arson there will be lots of origin points. If you want the investigators to believe this is deliberately set arson, you'll want to use multiple points.

Other indicators of arson are charring underneath furniture or door bottoms, which rarely happens in a natural blaze. Fire burning downward is also suspect, as is junk or papers stacked up around the place. The odors of flammable liquids may be detected by the well-trained nose of an investigator, or the bionic nose of a flammable vapor detection device.[2]

Plant enough realistic clues like this and you'll lead the investigators to believe exactly what you wish them to believe. For those truly interested in this subject, community colleges often offer courses in fire science which teach about arson investigation and procedures.

Switching the Blame

The investigators are going to look for motive when determining the cause of the fire. Therefore part of your cover-up should include a means of redirecting suspicion away from you, and onto somebody else. Fire investigators look for seven common motives when examining an arson site:

- Fraud;
- crime concealment;
- vanity;
- spite/revenge;
- pyromania;

- civil disorders, revolutions, political activities; and

- actions of juveniles, adolescents, and children.

Your goal is probably something along the lines of spite/revenge, but you wouldn't want the investigators thinking that, unless you can frame someone else as being out for revenge (such as an employee recently passed over for promotion). Instead you might want to try to convince authorities that crime concealment, pyromania, or juvenile delinquency was the motive.

There are two goals the arsonist should have in mind. Firstly, to take the blame for the fire away from the arsonist. This generally means switching blame to one of the final three groups of arsonists listed above, or may mean making the arson look like an accident. After all, an accidental fire, no matter how much one benefits from it, is still accidental. A second issue is the concealing of the true motivations for the fire.

To switch blame, you could drop clues in the vicinity that would point to a juvenile delinquent as the culprit. Let's say there's a convenience store nearby the business. You or one of your team members stakes out the convenience store, noticing any large groups of teens that come in and out. Let's say they all come out carrying Slurpees and cigarettes. Your team member goes into a different convenience store, makes identical purchases, then goes over to the arson site to plant the Slurpee cups and cigarettes near the scene. Over the next couple of days, investigators will come around to the convenience store questioning workers if they saw anything the night of the fire. Between the planted clues and the memory of the rowdy teens, the fire investigators will start piecing together what happened. It's them damned teenagers again!

(You could even have one of your team members follow the juveniles into the convenience store. After they leave, your team member goes up to the counter to make a purchase — and makes a nasty comment to the cashier, "There goes a bunch of juvenile offenders if I ever saw one." The statement may be true or not, but it will help cement the impression of rowdy teenagers in the mind of the cashier.)

How does one start a fire? The tendency is to throw a lot of gasoline everywhere, toss in a lighted match, and scram. That is both dangerous and easily detected as arson. When different substances burn, they give off distinct odors. The experienced fire fighter or investigator will recognize the smell of burning gasoline, and thus know the fire was pre-meditated arson. That's fine if you're plopping the blame on someone else's head, but if you want your fire to look like an accident, better stay away from obvious fire-starters like gasoline.

Fire is seen as a great all-encompassing machine that will eat whatever food it is given and leave behind nothing more than a useless paste of black filth. This is far from the truth. Many items — even highly flammable items — will survive a fire to some degree. For instance, the U.S. Federal Fire/Arson Detection Student Manual describes the result of a fire in a Michigan furniture store. The Fire Chief and others investigating the wreckage found two plastic containers of flammable liquid, burn marks in the carpet, pieces of tape, with burn marks and later, a piece of a fuse.[3] These are all items that one would expect would have been destroyed in the fire. We don't know if this fire in particular was arson, and we certainly don't know if the items were part of the cause or continuation of the fire. However, it is safe to conclude from this example (and many more like it) that the arsonist who uses special props like these can not count on the fire to eliminate them from the scene of the crime. Fire starters must either be left out, used with extreme caution, or must be innocent in nature, unless you want to create obvious arson.

Careless smoking is the most prevalent cause of residential fires, followed by:

- problems in electrical wiring

- heating/cooking equipment

- children playing with matches or lighters

- open flames and sparks

- flammable liquids

- suspected arson

- chimneys and flues

- lightning

- spontaneous ignition

Mrs. O'Leary's cow doesn't even make the top ten! So if you want to make it look like an accident, take care to finger one of these inanimate causes, like cigarettes or old wiring, as the culprit.

Before the Fire

Does the company have a smoke detector? A few days before the fire you'll want to remove the batteries. Or, better yet, put them in a Walkman and play music for hours until the batteries are as dead as you want that business to be. Then put them back in the smoke detector.

It would be terrible if the fire helps them collect a windfall in insurance money so they can rebuild and launch their business again. That's why you have to think this through beforehand. You could set up a fake insurance scam. Several months before, put on your business suit and an honest face, and convince the business owner that you have a great deal on insurance. Sell the owner your phony insurance, and when the fire rolls around a few months later, he'll be out of luck and uninsured. Another tactic: By intercepting the mail (Attacks #26 and #27) you can intercept checks meant for the insurance company. Also intercept the notices from the same insurance company asking why the hell they haven't paid up their insurance premiums. By the time their policy has been canceled, it's time to put on your big fiery show.

See if there is a way to subtly (or not-so-subtly) block entrances where fire fighters might try to come in to extinguish the blaze. Besides procrastinating their access it also casts suspicion that the fire was intentionally set.

The Big Frame Up

This fire thing is big, so might as well make the most of it. If you're going to start a fire you don't want to be standing in the line-up when it's all over. Better frame someone, such as some unfortunate executive recently passed over for promotion.

Investigators always look to see if any valuables were removed immediately before the fire. That's suspicious — it makes it look as though the fire was intentionally set to cover the theft. As part of your devious planning you'll want to steal some valuable stuff, like important papers, backup data, or one-of-a-kind models of upcoming products, and plant them on someone you're trying to frame. You could hide them in their backyard, or in the trunk of their car. After the fire, send an anonymous tip to the fire inspectors that you believe so-and-so spread the fire to cover his tracks.

You could start the fire soon after the guinea pig leaves work for the day (a common clue investigators look for to determine who set the place on fire). Another way to frame is to invite that person to a meeting at the company at that time of night, an hour or so after the fire has been given time to blaze its way through the building. The person will fit the common profile of the twisted arsonist who returns to view his work — and it will be too late by then for him to save anything from being wrecked in the fire.

If you didn't get around to canceling the owner's insurance or setting up your own phony insurance scam, you can make up for it by framing the business owner with the old insurance money ploy. Plant clues so the inspector will believe the business owner set it himself for the insurance money. Naturally they'll have no reason to suspect you, a mere innocent bystander in all this.

Citations

1. Sedaris, David. "Confessions of a Daytime Television Addict" in *The New York Times*. May 24, 1998. p. 31. David Sedaris's account of how he can't stay away from trashy daytime shows.
2. U.S. Federal Emergency Management Agency. *Student Guide For Fire/Arson Detection*. 1983. pp. 3-18 through

3-20. This student manual was the source for the list of common arson motivations as well as other information on fire investigations.

3. U.S. Federal Emergency Management Agency. pp. 6-6 and 6-7.

Your Plan of Attack

"People should just not vote, they should stop going to work, they should screech this whole fucking sham to a halt. Put the fuckers out of business and start all over again." — a very angry Sinéad O'Connor.

A business exists:

1. to make money, and

2. to fulfill a need or desire (the entrepreneur who has all-consuming passion).

It's your job to counteract those reasons. To make the business not profitable counteracts number 1. To mentally destroy the employees counteracts number 2. The business will fail when you have successfully, and repeatedly, counteracted these for a sustained length of time.

You can hurt them by: Turning their employees against them. Turning customers against them. Giving them annoying maintenance tasks to take care of that subtract from business goals (cleaning shit off walls). Making it too costly to do business. Wearing down their employees.

Your attacks may be public or anonymous. Environmental-type attacks are often publicized as a way of throwing light on the subject and gaining public support. This often backfires as the environmental group is made to look like poor losers. Might be better to stay anonymous in your attacks. Let the result of the attack (the poor customer relations that result, the lost sales) be publicized.

Start drawing together your team as you execute smaller attacks, and build your way up. Choose complementary attacks. Your attacks should be based on many issues. Some can be political (such as discrimination or animal testing) but also go for the non sequitur, the illogical mindless attacks, such as putting graffiti everywhere. You want to make them completely baffled and unable to respond, unable to guess your next move.

Pair up attacks to be more effective. When you spread rumors or contact the media, do that in conjunction with tying up their phone lines and faxes so customers and press can't have their concerns addressed.

Overcoming obstacles is difficult, but creating obstacles is easy. That's where you have the advantage. Money eventually wastes away. Energies wind down. Entropy wins. If you go at this hard enough, and forcefully enough, you're sure to win too.

YOU WILL ALSO WANT TO READ: